WOMEN'S VIEWS OF THE POLITICAL WORLD OF MEN

Edited by Judith Hicks Stiehm

 TRANSNATIONAL PUBLISHERS, INC.
Dobbs Ferry, New York

Most of these papers were prepared for the XII World Congress of the International Political Science Association held in Rio de Janeiro in August 1982. Royalties will be used to establish a travel fund for women attending future IPSA conferences.

Library of Congress Cataloging in Publication Data
Main entry under title:

Women's views of the political world of men.

Includes papers prepared for the 12th World Congress of the International Political Science Association, held in Rio de Janeiro in Aug. 1982.
    Bibliography: p.
    1. Women—Social conditions—Congresses.   2. Women—Legal status, laws, etc.—Congresses.   3. Political science—Congresses.   I. Stiehm, Judith.   II. International Political Science Association. World Congress (12th : 1982 : Rio de Janeiro, Brazil)
HQ1106.W665   1984   305.4'2   83-18041
ISBN 0-941320-22-7 (paper)

CONTENTS

1
INTRODUCTION

Judith Hicks Stiehm
University of Southern California
Los Angeles, California

The essays in this volume represent feminist explorations of Western political thought. They are trials, tests of the nature of Western tradition and of its value. They also represent a stage in an evolving scholarship. Only a decade ago women scholars discovered, first, the omission of women and then the appropriateness of women as subject. In examining the Western tradition for women as subject much was made of the implied and the oblique. For the most part, though, women as a subject remained the *object* of an analysis deeply imbued with a male perspective.

A second stage of scholarship sought to express women's views about themselves. This involved the development of self-consciousness and the formulation of concepts and theories rooted in self-knowledge and self-description.

These essays represent a third stage of scholarship. They are experiments in the treatment of men and their thought as objects of analysis. They are explorations of Western thought as the product of men's consciousness. They arise not from opposition or contradiction but from a new centeredness. The essays should prove valuable to both women and men, particularly men, for whom feminism can serve as a "looking-glass." It can do so (even though women refuse any longer to serve as men's "magnifying mirrors") by offering to men a view of the spot on the back of their heads. The allusions, of course, are to Virginia Woolf, who achieved this level of reflection before most of the authors included in this volume were born. Like Woolf, the authors are convinced that women must not surrender to mere antagonism, must not seek mere equality, and must not ignore the potential advantages, both intellectual and social, that marginality confers.

Each author has traditional political thought as her frame of reference. Within the literature of this thought much has been made of the distinction between the public and the private. Usually it has been implied that the public is the sphere of man and the private that of woman. Each author is aware of this antinomy, although not all accept its validity. After all, most men have only a meager public life while all have a private one. Further, women do not monopolize private life. Finally, the facts of each individual's private life do affect his/her public life and vice versa.

These essays come from a number of countries. They share the background of Western man's political thought, but they do not share a particular or ideological feminist tradition. No authoritative texts dominate these accounts. The authors rarely footnote one another. They do, however, complement and enrich one another's work.

In "Power as Ideology: A Feminist Analysis," Jane Jaquette argues that the definitions regularly used in Western political tradition serve to enhance male power while containing and dividing women. Drawing on the literature of anthropology and of economic development, Jaquette shows that [male] revolutionary and utilitarian theories offer little to women and that feminists must consider the consequences for both power and understanding of accepting theories which 1) divide the public from the private, and 2) fail to consider "nonpolitical," "noneconomic" woman.

The next two essays grew out of a consideration of two of the major problems created for women by their assignment to the private sphere. In "Overcoming the Barriers," Drude Dahlerup discusses the way in which women's issues have been (and are) kept from the public and formal political agendas. Her way of attacking the problem of nondecision-making is rooted in empirical political science. For her case study, Dahlerup takes the campaign for women's suffrage in Denmark during the nineteenth and twentieth centuries. Carole Pateman analyzes the effect of considering a public contract as analogous or relevant to that most intimate of private bonds—marriage. Drawing upon Mill and Hegel, Pateman argues in "The Shame of the Marriage Contract" that even feminist critiques of the marriage contract as insufficiently contractual lead to a shameful conclusion. However, because noncontractual bonds have led to subjection, she proposes a search for a new formulation which will accommodate a "differentiated social order" and provide "rich personal associations" for women and for men.

Fanny Tabak considers the special case of "Women and Authoritarian Regimes." Because these regimes are usually of military origin, women almost never participate in their governments. They do, however, both support and resist them. Tabak sees increased participation by women as crucial to any transition from authoritarian to democratic, from military to civilian government.

In her "Prologue to a Feminist Critique of War and Politics," Nancy Hartsock also considers the connection between the military and government. Drawing upon the *Iliad,* the *Oresteia* and Plato's *Symposium* and *Republic,* Hartsock examines the co-extensiveness of "man," "warrior," and "citizen." She explores the negativity of men's *eros* in a public world carefully separated from the private. Indeed, in the public world, she says, political action "is simply war by other means." Moreover, it is those means by which (male) citizens "attain and celebrate manhood."

Using Montesquieu's *Persian Letters* as illustrative material for "Despotism and Civil Society," Anna Yeatman extends Hartsock's analysis of the male–warrior–citizen by proposing a necessary connection between the apparent freedom and equality of the individual (male) participant in civil society and the despotic relations that same individual has with family members. Contract theory, Yeatman says, requires individuals who are free of particular dependencies; at the same time, individuals require the recognition of self which is offered by family members outside the civic system. In the past this has been accomplished for men through a gender division of labor. This has appeared workable because analysis, political theory, has been confined to consideration of the condition and status of one gender only— man's. Both Hartsock and Yeatman expose society's classic irony: that "free and equal" male citizens engage in a constant competition to establish themselves in a hierarchy rooted in force, while "subject and

5

inferior" private women participate in a web of familial relationships relatively free of both force and hierarchy.

In the last two essays, Lorenne Clark and I begin to consider "what is to be done." This assumes political theory is worth doing; it also assumes any theory must encompass the lives of women as well as men. Working within a Marxist framework, Clark describes class inequality as a development from sexual inequality and says Marxism must now develop a theory which provides for egalitarian relations of reproduction as it has already done for the relations of production. My essay has two principal themes. One deals with the special connection between men, government, and force, a theme found explicitly in the Tabak and Hartsock essays and implicitly in that of Jaquette. The second theme deals with human (men's and women's) connectedness—to family, to those around them, to other generations. This connectedness makes the individualistic social contract seem of dubious value. Similar views are developed in the Pateman, Yeatman and Clark essays. My approach, though, is like Dahlerup's—to attempt to grapple with what isn't there; in her case "what is not on the political agenda;" in my case "what is not explicit to the Western theoretical tradition." Thus my themes are developed around three unstated assumptions of men's theory: 1) that governments entail geography, not just people; 2) that people must be replaced and are sometimes *displaced*, but that governments should go on forever; and 3) that consent, deliberation and debate may be elements of some governments, but that there is no government without police and an army.

2
POWER AS IDEOLOGY:
A FEMINIST ANALYSIS

Jane S. Jaquette
Occidental College
Los Angeles, California

Power as Ideology:
A Feminist Analysis
Jane S. Jaquette

Power is one of the most over-studied concepts in political science, yet its modes and uses are still the subject of controversy. Is power a characteristic of a person or is it relational? Is it zero-sum or positive sum? Does the person on whom power is exercised partake in his/her own subjection? Is all exercise of power ultimately coercion?

These are the classic questions. The purpose of this paper is to resubject some of these issues to a feminist critique and to ask a new question: Is there an "ideology" of power? In other words, does the way we define power affect the way it is used and who can use it?[1]

The effect of such reanalysis should be to broaden our notions of what power is and how it works. First we will examine the conventional definitions of power. What we will find is that they define women out of the universe of political power holders and thus, in a very real way, out of politics itself. Further, women have traditionally accepted others' view that the power they experience is not "real" power; at best they may be "influential," and at worst "manipula-

1. Because we cannot treat the word "power" as a verb, power inevitably takes on properties of a substance "possessed" or "used" by individuals even though it is in fact clearly relational. For a discussion, see James N. Rosenau, "Capabilities and Control in an Interdependent World," in J. N. Rosenau, *The Study of Global Interdependence* (New York: Nichols Publishing Company, 1980), pp. 35ff.

tive." All female exercise of power, even in the private sphere, is thus denied legitimacy.

Revolutionary ideologies have the potential to diffuse power to new groups. I will argue that there is an important difference between women and other powerless groups. The revolutionary and liberationist ideologies that have galvanized politics in the post-colonial era can never fully mobilize women, in part because they fail to take into account the conflict between the domestic and public exercise of power in women's experience. For most women, the arena of public power is to be feared or avoided; politics is a "man's world." The effect of this split between public and private is that women are often the most opposed to their own liberation, as can be seen in the resistance of many women to the E.R.A. in the United States and also in the critique of feminism as inapplicable to Third World women.

Conventional Views of Power

In a recent review of the literature on power, Dennis Wrong[2] divides the forms of power into four categories: coercion, authority, manipulation, and persuasion. If these are ordered hierarchically from the most to the least feared, we can see that women are least likely to have access to the means of coercion and most likely to possess the capacity to persuade. Authority is less likely to be attributed to women than to men, in either political or interpersonal contexts. The ability to manipulate is very commonly attributed to women, although often in an attempt to deny its legitimacy or effectiveness. Persuasion is the weakest form of power, yet women's access even to this mild form of power is not fully accepted. Until recently women have been enjoined to be as silent in politics as in church.

---

2. Dennis Wrong, *Power: Its Forms, Bases and Uses* (New York: Harper and Row, 1979). I have used Wrong's thorough and fascinating review of the types of power and authority to provide the categories for the first half of this paper. See especially Chapters 2 and 3. For other recent works, see also James T. Tadeschi, *Perspectives on Social Power* (Chicago: Aldine Publishing Co., 1974), and Stewart Clegg, *Power, Rule and Domination* (London: Routledge and Kegan Paul, 1975).

Coercion

For realists and neo-Machiavellians, coercion is the only true form of power; any other form is either fraud or deceit.[3] Forms of power are conceptually distinguished by the different ways in which those who accede to power comply; in this case the distinction is made between the use or threat of physical force and the "deception" of authority, manipulation or persuasion. Women do not generally have access to the means of coercion. In the dyadic male/female relationship, the standard justification of male institutional power is often—illogically—derived from the ability of the individual male to overpower the individual female.[4] Until very recently, women were denied any role in the coercive institutions of society, the military and the police. It is clear that any definition of power that rests on force alone will exclude women as power holders.

It would seem strange, or inappropriate, or pointless, to most women even to think of challenging the male monopoly on the means of coercion, even though there is no logical reason why they could not do so. An ideology which challenged the existing male monopoly on violence and made it seem right for women to hold power could make a significant difference in the sexual distribution of this capability.[5] That men can also imagine this is at the base of recurring male fears of matriarchy: "Don't let them do unto us as we've done unto them."

---

3. Wrong, *op. cit.* pp. 84–85.

4. This is a classic "level of analysis" problem. Women could band together to overcome males, particularly in this era of high technology, and thus reverse the roles, just as a few men, who could easily be physically overpowered by those they rule, can seize control of a given society. Thus to some degree women's powerlessness in this arena is not self-evident; it depends on existing forms of social organization. Historically, women have banded with men against other groups led by men.

5. See Judith Stiehm, *Bring Me Men and Women* (Berkeley: Univ. of California Press, 1981). For two sympathetic accounts of female power written by men, see Philip E. Slater, *The Glory of Hera* (Boston: Beacon Press, 1971), and David C. McClelland, "Power and the Feminine Role," in his *Power: The Inner Experience* (New York: John Wiley and Sons, 1975).

Authority

The different forms of power outlined by Wrong are interdependent. He notes that the forms under which a given regime is established are likely to change over time.[6] Coercive power has a tendency to become power based on authority. Authority wards off constant challenges to the threat of force; the use of force is expensive, and no regime can stay in power if it is based solely on coercion. Yet, as we shall see, women are also largely excluded from the category of holders of authority.

Authority as a concept is almost as complex as power itself. "Legitimate" authority connotes the acceptance within a social community that a given individual has the "right to command" by virtue of being in a particular role. Thus it is distinguished from "personal" authority based on the qualities of the person. Legitimate authority is based on shared community norms, ultimately backed by the community's ability to punish those who disobey.[7]

When we examine access to legitimate authority, we find that, although women are increasingly represented in the labor force, in "male" professions, as voters and as activist citizens, they have yet to make much of a dent in the male domination of political elite roles.[8] Definitions of power which focus on legitimate authority and formal elite roles will include few women, and those women are still exceptions to the rule. Anthropology shows us that by and large women have always been excluded from the formal or ritual aspects of the exercise of power,[9] although there are some notable exceptions, as among the Iroquois, where women were tribal elders. There does seem to be some evidence that the exclusion of women increases as

---

6. Wrong, *op. cit.,* Ch. 5.

7. *Ibid.,* p. 51.

8. See Sandra Baxter and Marjorie Lansing, *The Invisible Majority* (Ann Arbor: University of Michigan Press, 1980), and Jane S. Jaquette, ed., *Women in Politics* (New York: John Wiley and Sons, 1974).

9. See Peggy Sanday, "Female Status in the Public Domain," in Michele Z. Rosaldo and Louise Lamphere, *Women, Culture and Society* (Stanford, Calif.: Stanford University Press, 1974), pp. 189–206.

the state becomes differentiated as a separate institution in society.[10] Eleanor Leacock has argued that women dominated the economy when the household and the economy were one and the same,[11] but that female economic power declines as the economy becomes more differentiated. Similarly, the fact that economic, social, and political functions were combined in tribal organization suggests that women, particularly older women, had significantly more power before the rise of the state.

This whole discussion, however, ignores the fact that women are enforcers of community norms, the fundamental guides to behavior in traditional and tribal societies. Political science conventionally distinguishes "social control" from "legitimate" authority, arguing, as Wrong does, that social control rests on internalized norms and not on the external exercise of power through authority.[12] This has the effect of defining the most common form of female power—the ability to punish deviation from social norms—as "not-power." It should be recognized however that, even in traditional societies obedience does not result from internalized rules alone. It involves many of the characteristics of power exercise: the threat of sanction, the tendency to "make an example of" deviants, and, as in the case of totalitarian systems, an invasion of "private space." The family is not a refuge from the "public" sphere in this instance, but an extension of it. Social control conforms to other characteristics of modern political power as defined by Bertrand de Jouvenel: it is "comprehensive" (it applies to a range of acts) and "extensive" (few if any members of the society are exempt from its control).[13]

---

10. In the work of anthropologists Sherry Ortner and June Nash.

11. Eleanor Leacock, "Women's Status in Egalitarian Society: Implications for Social Evolution," *Current Anthropology* IX (June 1978), p. 250.

12. Wrong, *op. cit.,* writes (p. 3): "When social controls have been internalized, the concept of power as a social relation is clearly inapplicable, but to assume that most conformity to norms is the result of internalization is to adopt what I have called an 'over-socialized conception' of man."

13. Quoted in Wrong, *op. cit.,* pp. 14–15. De Jouvenel also sees "intensivity" as an attribute of power, when "the bidding of A can be pushed far without loss of compliance." This would seem to hold for social control

I am dwelling on these comparisons because I think that women are the main arbiters and enforcers of this form of legitimate authority. Social control is partially replaced by the rule of law as societies become more complex, and is not replaced by other forms of legitimate power for women. This process closely parallels Esther Boserup's evidence on the impact of modernization on women's *economic* roles.[14] But it is also interesting to explore possible differences between power, as conventionally defined, and social control. What is the "sanction" behind this kind of power? It is not direct physical coercion, although the overt violation of certain taboos led in the past to physical consequences such as stoning or time in the stocks. The operative threat would seem to be banishment or social isolation and loss of status. Hobbes' definition of power is interesting in this context, for Hobbes argues that power is the "present means to any future apparent good." In a "traditional" or even semi-modern context, status (reputation) is required for social advancement or to ensure continued acceptance in the community, a present means to a future good. At the margin—that is, at the margin where the individual consciously wishes to deviate but does not do so for fear of social sanction—this kind of power conforms to the conventional modern definition as well, that A has power over B if A can make B do something he/she would not otherwise do.[15]

In the final analysis social control has been dealt the most severe blow not by law but by liberal individualism. This suggests a significant difference between power as we now conceive of it and social control. The standard model assumes that A, whether operating under the constraints of legitimate authority or with unlimited access to the means of coercion, can choose from a wide range of behaviors to ask of B.[16] In the case of social control there is relatively little room to maneuver; the social rules are known and females enforce those rules re-

---

when viewed from the standpoint of B's expectations of "individual freedom" in a liberal society; yet A does not have the arbitrary choices of what to ask of B that are implied by intensivity.

14. Esther Boserup, *Women's Role in Economic Development* (London: George Allen & Unwin, Ltd., 1970).

15. As in Max Weber's formulation, or Robert Dahl's.

16. From Hobbes onward through Dahl, et al.

acting as a group, not as power-maximizing individuals (although there is some latitude in deciding what constitutes a violation or an appropriate punishment). Social control puts in sharp relief some of the assumptions of the standard model. What is the significance of treating power as a line of force between A and B, a single relation between two individuals isolated from the rest of society? If power were seen instead as resulting in a set of behaviors over time, embedded in a network of social interactions, it would approach the complexity of the phenomenon in the real world. Social control, peer sanctions and reputation are still important determinants of behavior, but women seem to play less of a role than they did when the social and political spheres overlapped more.

We have reviewed legitimate authority, but there are other forms worth at least a brief examination: personal authority (as defined earlier), authority by inducement (you obey the boss because he pays you), and competent authority (you obey someone because he/she knows more and conforming to that knowledge will make you better off).

Charisma is the standard example of *personal authority,* and at least one scholar takes the view that women are incapable of having or imparting charisma,[17] one more reason why women do not or cannot hold political power. In one sense this is simple to refute by example: it would be hard to argue, it seems to me, that successful political women from Indira Gandhi to Evita Peron have not had some measure of that elusive quality. Is female charisma different in some key respects from male charisma? The logical distinction is that women have charisma based on idealized feminine roles (Evita's image as a *patrona,* a source of nurturance and welfare for her *descamisados*), but it is harder to imagine women as charismatic military figures or as statesmen, although Golda Meir and Margaret Thatcher might provide counter-examples. The more women can be observed holding high public office, the less likely such generalizations will hold.

At the micro-level, a common example of personal authority is that of the loved one; the fact that the lover will often do things which are "irrational" or against his own best interests out of love is seen as an

---

17. Lionel Tiger; see also Weber's discussion of charisma.

interesting example of power based on personal qualities of a particular individual. A look at the micro-level provokes some unexpected questions, however. It may well be true, as Constantina Safilios-Rothschild argues,[18] that a woman's strategy for achieving power in marriage is based on what she calls the "love debt," namely to marry a man who is much more in love with her than she with him. But I think it is impossible to argue that the "love debt" is the ongoing basis of power relationships in marriage, however successful the female was in insuring an original "exchange rate" favorable to her interests. Just as Wrong argues that personal power does not survive close scrutiny ("no one is a hero to his valet"), so I would argue that the "love debt" does not explain the ordinary politics of marriage.

It is not that the love debt is irrelevant: "love," or protestations of love, may become an important item of exchange for other goods (money, household services, cooperation) between the two parties and may even be the basis upon which a given man or woman rationalizes subjecting his/her will ("I really don't want to take out the garbage") to another ("but I'll do it anyway"). One way of looking at the love debt would be to compare it to Theodore Moran's[19] ratchet model for the distribution of power between multinational corporations and host countries: the lover is willing to give up a great deal to secure the commitment of the loved one, just as the host country may offer tax and other concessions to the MNC to attract new investment. But after the investment is made and the MNC has its assets invested (a situation comparable to the loved one taking herself off the marriage market), then the host country can "tighten the screws" without fear of the MNC's withdrawing. This dynamic continues until the point where the country wishes to encourage a major new investment on the part of the MNC and then, Moran argues, the process begins again at a higher level. As the marriage settles into a normal as opposed to an enamored state, the loved one would continue to lose power un-

18. Constantina Safilios-Rothschild, "A Macro- and Micro-Examination of Family Power and Love," *Journal of Marriage and the Family* XXXVIII (May 1976), pp. 355–362.

19. Theodore Moran, *Multinational Corporations and the Politics of Dependence* (Princeton, N.J.: Princeton University Press, 1974).

less a means could be found to activate the ratchet—jealousy, perhaps, or consent to have children, or failure to provide a supportive home environment.

Otherwise, the power arrangements in marriage collapse into social control (in traditional societies the man would have some incentive to keep the marriage together and working to maintain his social status), authority by inducement (here the male usually has all the economic levers, although it may be socially unacceptable to use them, and the woman has sex or cooperation to give or withhold), or physical coercion. Both may operate on shared goals (although agreement on such goals may not be purely voluntary) that the husband and wife could each exercise power within different but complementary spheres (what Theodore Geiger calls "intercursive" power[20]). Both may "cooperate," that is, each may exchange compliance according to some pattern usually worked out by trial and error. B behaves as A would like this time in order that A will concede next time or in the future. This is an ongoing game of reciprocal concessions, although the pattern may reveal power assymmetry between the husband and wife.

The ability to grant or withhold rewards is authority by *inducement,* a common form of power which, if exercised in a context of extremely unequal access to resources, is exploitation. Inducements can be seen either as material or non-material rewards, and one of the major reasons why marriage has been attacked as a male-dominated institution by feminists since the mid-nineteenth century is the unequal distribution of material resources between men and women in most marriages. This imbalance is perpetuated by social control: men lose status by being "kept" by wealthy wives and forbid their wives from working or keeping separate financial accounts.

As I noted earlier, older women in tribal societies were thought to have "wisdom," a form of *competent authority.* Insofar as competence in a modern society is linked to mastery of science and technology, or even the "sciences" of economics or politics, we find women greatly underrepresented in these fields and in careers which are based on these skills. Instead, female competence is seen as legitimate

---

20. Discussed in J. A. A. Van Doorn, "Sociology and the Problem of Power, cited in Wrong, *op. cit.,* p. 260n.

and credible largely when women stick to jobs related to their stereotypical roles—as nurturers and educators—and not as scientists, engineers, or public administrators. This in turn reflects a split in our culture between science and the humanities, between "skills" and experience, between the doers and the thinkers. In our technological age, women are even less likely to be perceived as competent than as charismatic.[21]

Manipulation and Persuasion

The two remaining forms of power, manipulation and persuasion, are conceptually different. In *manipulation,* B acts according to A's goals without knowing it, and in persuasion, A convinces B it is in his/her interest to act in conformity with A's goals. But they are similar in an important respect for the purposes of this analysis.

The striking fact is that, although the capacity to persuade or manipulate is more readily attributed to women than authority or coercive power, these "female" capacities when attributed to women, are seen to operate exclusively in the private sphere. It could be argued that women resort to manipulation of their husbands or children because they lack authority or a credible threat of force even in "their" sphere; thus manipulation is not a typically "female" form of power "by nature," as is often asserted, but is a direct result of their powerlessness.

Persuasion in the hands of women linked to influential men can be a significant public sphere resource (e.g., courtesans and presidents' wives). Yet it is not a reliable resource, even in the private sphere. Insofar as persuasion is the art of reason—that is, the ability of A to convince B that he/she should do something because of "objective" consequences that apply regardless of A's will—then persuasion is based on "better" knowledge or "better" application of cause-effect reason-

---

21. For a literary treatment of the opposite theme—that women's wisdom is practical and science is impractical alchemy—see Gabriel Garcia Marquez, *One Hundred Years of Solitude.* Dorothy Dinnerstein links the Oedipal Complex to the development of technology and its inexorable logic in *The Mermaid and the Minotaur: Sexual Arrangements and the Human Malaise* (New York: Harper-Colophon, 1977).

ing by A, and "success" in convincing B of that fact. It is a common-place of feminist critiques of marriage that men use "reason" and women use "emotion"—and men usually win.[22] Men have access to the knowledge and rhetorical techniques of the public sphere to help them win these battles, and women's relative isolation works against them.

It is possible, indeed likely, that female persuasion in the male/female power relation will depend instead on threats of withdrawal of cooperation, emotional escalation, and denial of sex—all "sanctions" within the woman's control, providing the marriage or relationship continues. This is "the politics of everyday marriage," what John Stuart Mill criticized when he argued that women should be encouraged to seek "liberty" (full citizenship) in the public sphere rather than subject their families to the negative effects of power exercised in the home.[23] Mill argued that "liberty" and "power" are opposite forces, which can be debated,[24] but that power is corrosive when exercised in a confined space seems clear.[25]

Turning now to the public sphere, we see that women are not more successful or more likely than men to use manipulation or persuasion, although in contrast to the means of coercion they are not totally denied access to these resources. It is no accident that the battle of the early feminists was the battle for the right to speak publicly, and there are poignant parallels between the writings of Sor Juana Inez de la Cruz and Angelina Grimke on this question.[26] Insofar as persuasion requires access to information, the capacity to know and to attack the

---

22. John Scanzoni, *Sexual Bargaining; Power Politics in the American Marriage* (Englewood Cliffs, N.J.: Prentice Hall, 1972).

23. As discussed in Jean Bethke Elshtain, *Public Man, Private Woman* (Princeton: Princeton University Press, 1981), p. 138.

24. See Hannah Arendt discussed in Steven Lukes, *Power: A Radical View* (London: Macmillan, 1974), p. 30ff.

25. See also the discussion in Kate Millett, *Sexual Politics* (Garden City, New York: Doubleday, 1970).

26. See Helene Cixous, "The Laugh of the Medusa," in Elaine Marks and Isabelle de Courtivron, eds., *The New French Feminisms* (New York: Schocken Books, 1981).

status quo through the formulation of new ideology, women have largely been absent from those arenas as well. Where are our women political theorists, our social critics, our think tank analysts inventing the future? It is here of course that equal access to education and to jobs can make a visible difference. In the political arena per se, however, women still have difficulty competing on an equal footing with men. Persuasion in politics means money, not just ideas or charisma, and women are still unable to command financial support for their campaigns.

Power, Women, and Revolutionary Ideologies

Because an asymmetrical pattern of distribution of wealth and resources is the starting point for political mobilization, at least in the 20th century where inequality has become the primary focus of politics,[27] parallels between the position of women and other oppressed groups have served as important examples for the feminist movement. Under conditions of a high degree of inequality, the powerless share important characteristics: They are not only poor, they are also isolated from each other, lack class consciousness (i.e., knowledge of their "real" interests), and are subject to negative sanctions if they attempt to unite to overthrow the system.

One model of powerlessness, the patron/client model,[28] which shows the isolation of each peasant from other peasants and the dependence (of each peasant in competition with others) on the landlord, is suggestive to feminists of how marriage works. Women are "poor;" that is, they lack their own resources; they are highly dependent on a single individual for material support and even for human companionship and reinforcement of self-image and they are discour-

---

27. But for a theoretical counterargument in the case of women, see Elizabeth H. Wolgast, *Equality and the Rights of Women* (Ithaca, N.Y.: Cornell University Press, 1980).

28. See, for example, George M. Foster, "The Dyadic Contract: A Model for the Social Structure of a Mexican Village," in Steffan W. Schmidt, et al (eds.), *Friends, Followers and Factions: A Reader in Political Clientelism* (Berkeley: University of California Press, 1977), pp. 15–27.

aged by a variety of factors from uniting together to overthrow male domination.

Despite other parallels that are quite disturbing between the structure of marriage and the structure of peasant/landlord relations, and despite attempts by the feminist movement to focus on marriage as a male-dominated power institution which isolates women from each other, a feminist movement cannot be compared to a peasant revolution. The peasant can improve his situation by eliminating the landlord and taking his land. For women, the elimination of men is hardly an optimal strategy. At this stage, at least, the strategy of becoming "like men," that is, of acquiring the skills, opportunities and incomes of men, appears to be the only option. Tearing down the existing structure of power in a violent revolution would leave less rather than more to go around. The goal is not the control of an outside resource but a change in the way emotional and economic goods are both produced and shared.

One reason why women do not overthrow marriage as an exploitative institution is the fact that they are not fully powerless within it: as noted earlier, they have some resources to offer in exchange for male resources. For many women the "bargain" they can achieve in marriage significantly exceeds the material and non-material rewards they could achieve by "exit" from a given marriage or by destroying the institution.

As women increasingly have access to economic resources outside marriage (and this may vary by class, with women at the highest and lowest ends of the class structure capable of earning incomes equal to males of their class), the incentive to stay within a marriage in which the male exercises power inappropriate to that underlying distribution of economic resources declines. The weakening of social mores favoring marriage and constraining men to act "as good husbands," the decline of alimony laws, and the pulling apart of extended families, all of which in the past gave women positive leverage within marriage, will interact to increase the tendency for women to choose "exit" over "voice" or "loyalty." This in turn may cause men to concede more to keep their wives married to them, counteract the decline of traditional sources of female power within marriage, or produce a pattern of serial marriage. It is unlikely that "marriage" (in the sense of

21

male/female dyads) will cease to function as the most common form of male/female relations, though the power distribution within these dyads will show a high degree of variability.

There is one other interesting parallel worth noting here. It is not only women who lack access to the "higher" forms of power—so do most men, and, to take a very different example, so do small states in the international system.[29] There are two different kinds of responses to perceived power asymmetries. The "oppressed" are those who give up the comforts of the status quo and engage in revolutionary activity—band together, develop a counter ideology, and attempt to overthrow the system. They either recognize their *potential* power or gain strength from hopelessness. By contrast, the "weak" have no hope of overthrowing the system; they see short- or medium-term benefits from continued participation, using a variety of strategies to enhance their claims. They rely on laws to protect themselves against the use of force and press for changes in the rules of the game to favor smaller players. They use persuasion, that is, the development of ideologies or sets of symbols which constrain the behavior of the more powerful actors, and engage in boycotts.

Radical feminism, with its threat of separatism, has been the source of revolutionary ideology within the modern feminist movement. But, as a practical matter, most women cannot easily opt to be "self-reliant" any more than poor economies can easily band together and withdraw from the international system. Thus we should expect to find—and do find—that feminist strategies and the strategies of small states are similar.

From the analysis presented above I think it is possible to draw at least four major conclusions. First, women clearly have less access than men to power resources, including the resources necessary to achieve the various forms of authority. Second, the attempt to draw parallels between macro-views of power and the microcosm of male/female relations (or between the "public" and "private" spheres as feminist writers would label them) shows some surprising similari-

29. See Robert L. Rothstein, *Alliances and Small Powers* (New York: Columbia University Press, 1968), and Elizabeth Janeway, *Powers of the Weak* (New York: Knopf, 1980).

ties and suggests that the terms power and politics are applicable at the micro-level. Third, despite structural similarities between these levels, it is also clear that women's domestic sphere power is like a "soft" currency in the international economy; it appears to be inconvertible into public sphere power. Fourth, a closer look at the micro-level indicates that, despite the mainstream feminist critique of the family as a male-dominated and exploitative institution, women have power resources that the feminist critique, which is based on public sphere criteria, often underestimates. What is the basis for female rejection of revolutionary models? How does women's private sphere experience both bar and alienate them from political life and full citizenship?

The Inconvertibility of Female Power: Implications for the Public Sphere

The concept of inconvertibility suggests what I think is one of the most important characteristics of power as women customarily exercise it. Manipulative and persuasive exercises of power by women do not easily translate into the public arena. Further, there may even be a zero-sum relationship between power capabilities inside the home and the requirements for exercising power outside the home, e.g., strong public norms have argued against women running for office (because they would neglect their families). Women must still prove that their families are well taken care of and that they are not opposed to the family as an institution in order to be credible candidates.

But these difficulties can be overcome. The problem of effective female participation in politics—full citizenship—goes much deeper. Juliet Mitchell and Nancy Chodorow have shown us that gender differences are caused by factors much more intractable than mere socialization.[30] I would argue that the failure of women to participate fully in politics is not only that they experience "role conflict," but that they are alienated from the process, and to a lesser degree from

---

30. Nancy Chodorow, *The Reproduction of Mothering* (Berkeley: University of California Press, 1978). Juliet Mitchell, *Psychoanalysis and Feminism* (Harmondsworth, England: Penguin, 1976).

the goals, of politics. Quite apart from the question of whether women are "allowed" to expand their horizons beyond the domestic, I would argue that women are put off from the public sphere because it fails to conform in key ways to expectations and values they have achieved in the domestic sphere and that they do not want to sacrifice for the uncertain rewards of the public sphere. In part the rewards are uncertain because women don't have the power to get what they want in the public sphere, and thus they are repeatedly negatively reinforced. But in part I think it can also be argued that the content of politics—what is up for negotiation—is not of interest to many women. They don't have a *stake* in politics.[31]

In addition I would argue that the "stuff" of politics, the process of bargaining and negotiation, what counts as "wins" and "losses," and the atmosphere in which this takes place are alienating to women. I am not just talking about the "rough and tumble" or the "smoke-filled rooms" or the competition; there are many women who thrive on these things. I am referring to what I see as a deep sense on the part of many women that politics is irrelevant or corrupt, that the public arena is not the *res publica* envisioned by Hannah Arendt, but a kind of male sand-box; activities which men from Homer and Aristotle on have regarded highly are seen by women as useless or beside the point.[32]

An interesting example is that when issues of dependency or the conflict between the PLO and Israel intruded into the U.N. Decade for Women meetings in Mexico City and Copenhagen, many women objected to the "politicizing" of the meetings. Of course, this position was considered with the interest of the United States in keeping such concerns off the agenda, but that is not the point. For U.S. feminists, it would appear that there is a "male politics," but women debating policies and distributive agendas at U.N. meetings are engaged in some other form of activity. This view was not limited to feminists; the male press seemed to think that what would happen when women got together would be "different," and women were ridiculed for engaging in conflict instead of "rising above" it.

---

31. See discussion in Jane S. Jaquette, "Introduction," *op. cit.*

32. *On Revolution* (New York: Viking Press, 1961).

Although she denied being a feminist, I think it is not irrelevant that it was Hannah Arendt who championed the public sphere in a way that cleansed it of some of its more objectionable qualities—its modern preoccupation with economic inequality to the exclusion of other values and the devaluation of political discourse.[33] Similarly, I find her description of power congruent with a female perspective: "Power and violence are opposites; where one rules absolutely, the other is absent"[34]—a total rejection of the neo-Machiavellian equation of power with force, but not one that denies coercion as a factor in politics.

Even socialism, which replaces "bourgeois" politics[35] with community (the family idealized), has not bridged the gap. I have argued elsewhere that communist parties have not appealed broadly to women, despite active recruitment efforts, because they are perceived by them as displacing the family, attacking religion, and altering the pattern of daily interactions. In socialist theory, private sphere activities are "socialized;" women are liberated through work and political activity. It is not surprising that many women find this vision less than compelling, just as many women have resisted the E.R.A.

Rethinking Power

I have some thoughts on how a reconceptualization of power might be undertaken which would bring the notion of power closer to the female experience of it, and in doing so make it possible to restructure politics as well. What is the effect of thinking about the parallel between power and money? With power as a kind of currency, social relations can be seen as "market" relations, and individuals wield power to maximize utility. This suggests one way to describe the incompatibility between women's lives and political involvement.

When I used the term "inconvertibility" of female power, I bor-

---

33. In *The Human Condition* (Chicago: University of Chicago Press, 1958).

34. Quoted in Wrong, *op. cit.*, p. 26.

35. E.g., C. B. MacPherson's analysis in *The Real World of Democracy* (New York: Oxford University Press, 1966).

rowed Talcott Parson's image of power as credit, an expanding money (or capability) supply that can be used to control nature or expand (community) resources. This view is sharply contrasted to the zero-sum view of power as a finite resource, a limited good.[36] These conflicting images have become part of the "pluralist/elitist" debate and the radical critique of structural-functionalism,[37] but I do not want to debate the revolutionary and counter-revolutionary implications of these opposing metaphors here. Instead I would like to suggest that viewing power as currency is not simply consistent with a status-quo-oriented idealism as its critics suggest, but also allows us to focus on the rational calculus of power based on "realist" assumptions of competitive individualism.

Conventionally economic and game theoretical views of politics concentrate on the *voter* as a maximizer of utilities in order to predict or explain certain political outcomes. I think it would be useful to move to another level: how does this image square with what women experience in the domestic arena? Do women make marginal calculations to maximize their utility, choosing among a kind of smorgasbord of economic and political goods? Or are the goods of the domestic arena more clustered, "stickier" (less divisible) in a way that makes the smorgasbord analogy seem as strange for them as it is for the poor who haven't the wherewithal to get into the cafeteria? Marginal utility and market analogies are ubiquitous in modern thought. How well do they conform to the ordering principles of male and female reality?

In everyday experience, males impose order by focus, by control over their schedules and tasks (assembly line work is alienating precisely because this does not occur), and by separating themselves from the home; they seek disorder through adventure. Politics combines those two sides of male existence. By contrast, I would argue, women's daily lives are naturally chaotic; they achieve order not in time or space but at the emotional level. Chaos is tamed by domestic coalition-building or controlled by the imposition of emotional sanctions. By and large, the options available for political participation are

---

36. Talcott Parsons, *Politics and Social Structure* (New York: The Free Press, 1969).

37. See Steven Lukes, *op. cit.*

not congruent with these needs, although we do find greater participation by women in areas which are more so—e.g., campaign work (often a solidarity activity with other women) and in groups committed to "causes" (e.g., environmental groups).

Yet another line of inquiry suggested by the currency metaphor is to use it to reexamine "traditional" authority. Dennis Wrong argues that obeying traditional authority is irrational because it requires that individuals act against their (economic) interests.[38] By implication, women are also irrational in their traditionalism, in their refusal to become individuals (social atoms?) in the modern sense. Yet it can be argued that "tradition" is rational when it functions to minimize risks over the long term, as James C. Scott argues in *The Moral Economy of the Peasant*.[39] The analogous calculation for women would be that male dominance in the public sphere is and has been historically greater than in the private sphere. Given long-term female exclusion from the public sphere, marriage, despite its exploitative characteristics, is a "rational" choice in Scott's sense. Women do contribute to the construction of their social worlds; to assume they are waiting to be freed from their chains is romantic, but unrealistic, as Jean Elshtain notes when she writes that:

> The liberal feminist devaluation of the private sphere and the woman's place within it is a curious thing. On the one hand, it involves a recognition of ongoing social realities, as families are less and less "havens in a heartless world" and all that implies. But to reduce motherhood to a "role" is to speed up and enhance the process of eroding the private sphere and its relations of their significance and value, with nothing, one must point out, to take its place.[40]

Albert Hirschman's provocative study of the transition between traditional and modern values[41] argues that capitalism created the condi-

---

38. Wrong, *op. cit.*

39. James C. Scott, *The Moral Economy of the Peasant* (New Haven: Yale University Press, 1976).

40. Elshtain, *op. cit.*, p. 243.

41. Albert O. Hirschman, *The Passions and the Interests* (Princeton, N.J.: Princeton University Press, 1977).

tions for social order by pitting the "interests" against the more dangerous "passions," particularly the passions of rulers, but also activities further down the social scale. Pursuit of individual economic interests—creating a "nation of shopkeepers"—is far less threatening to the body politic, the pursuit of power, or other "passionate" goals, including revolutionary change.

Yet what are the "interests" of women? Are women's goals amenable to the utilitarian calculus? Or are they, like value issues, not amenable to pluralist distributive politics? Is liberal capitalist practice—with its focus on economic issues, recurring rounds of interest articulation and interest aggregation, and its suspicion of political passions—unsatisfying to women (and ultimately to men)? This line of analysis also finds a parallel in feminist theory. Dorothy Dinnerstein criticizes male use of "rational" technology to dominate the physical world, with ultimately negative consequences for the environment and for the quality of life.[42] But can we move in a counter direction without idealizing the past or moving toward totalitarianism?

Conclusion

If feminists succeed in convincing a majority of women that they can act as "economic men" and, through the use of law, persuasion, and growing economic clout prevent the norms and the institutions of society from pushing them back into "their place," then the questions I am trying to raise here are moot. We will have "won." However, I am not convinced we will win, even on these terms, or that the victory will be worth the cost. I am convinced that any "feminist" revolution needs to take the day-to-day needs and interests of women as women into account. This cannot be done by assuming that all women will eventually become like the elite woman professional; instead, it must take into account the realities of poverty and powerlessness. Lifelong persistence of asymmetrical male/female relations is the single most important fact of life for most women.

Most feminist strategies of change have emphasized egalitarian

---

42. Dinnerstein, *op. cit.*

politics and I would not belittle such efforts nor argue, as some have, that they have had little effect. I see a dramatic change in the range of options open to American women and expect that international feminism, independent of U.S. views and experiences, will continue to progress to the benefit of women who are experiencing the abrupt loss of power and reduced access to independent resources that accompany modernization.

What I am suggesting is something different: that we take the evidence of the resistance of some women to their own "liberation" as an opportunity to rethink our goals, not to acquiesce in the traditional power relations between males and females, but to try to redefine power—and thus politics—in ways that enhance the humanity of both.

3
OVERCOMING THE BARRIERS:
AN APPROACH TO HOW WOMEN'S
ISSUES ARE KEPT FROM THE
POLITICAL AGENDA

Drude Dahlerup
University of Aarhus
Aarhus, Denmark

Overcoming the Barriers
Drude Dahlerup

Introduction

Women's social position has never been a major issue in Western public policy. The organizations as well as the political institutions are structured on the basis of other conflict-dimensions. Public policy concerning women has generally not owned public institutions of its own. The interest of women and the conflicts between men and women are, as everyone can see, not institutionalized into a sector with its own department, its minister, boards and commissions—and established formal and informal contacts between the public authorities and some well-established interest organizations that could claim to be representatives for some well-defined interests. Nothing like that has ever existed. The Women's Status Commissions, the Equal Status Councils and the like, which have been established very recently in most Western countries, represent a very new—and very modest— feature.

The political parties always seem to have avoided politicizing issues concerning women's position. Consensus rather than conflict between the male political elites on "the woman question" has characterized the political systems during the last one hundred years.

Original version presented at ECPR/IPSA joint workshop on "The Political Socialization of Men and Women," Lancaster, England, 1981.

33

Two waves of legislation aimed at furthering the equality of men and women can be identified in most Western countries. The first wave came about 1900–1920; the second in the 1970s and 1980s. But even in these periods, public policy towards women was not one of the salient issues of the political scene.

To study public policy towards women therefore implies an analysis not only of actual decisions, but also of silence, of nondecisions. How do you study such "non-issues?" How are women's position, equality between the sexes, women's emancipation or whatever we are talking about (see "What are Women's Issues," below) kept off the political agenda?

This paper will develop a scheme for studying *agenda-building* concerning issues on which nondecision-making is more usual than decision-making. In the last part of the paper, I will use the scheme in a case study of women's suffrage in Denmark.

The present deliberations are part of a larger project of mine entitled "Women's Liberation/Equality as a Political Issue in Danish Politics 1870 until Today." The project also consists of a study of the actual public policy towards women during the entire period and an analysis of the ideology, perception of reality, role, and strategy of: 1) the political parties, and 2) a selected number of women's organizations. This paper is limited to the question of how issues are raised to or suppressed from the political agenda. I will discuss neither the outcome nor the implementation of the cases. If the concepts of nondecision-making, mobilization of bias, issue creation, and issue suppression can ever be made useful, the non-issue of women's social position ought to be an obvious case.

The Biased Political System

That Western political systems do not function the way the pluralists thought is now a well-established fact. The political system in the Western liberal democracies (and in all other political systems as well) is biased. Not only do large groups of people never participate in the political process, but issues are also systematically excluded from serious consideration by the political system. And the outcome suits the interest of certain groups better than that of others. Gamson speaks about "stable unrepresentation."[1] Schattschneider has formulated it this way: "Some issues are organized into politics while others are organized out."[2] Helga Maria Hernes says that "By creating institutions that take care of essential values a state and a society signals which values it wants to advance, to preserve, and to create."[3] One could add: "and which conflicts it considers necessary to control by institutionalizing them."

The very important concept of *nondecision-making* has been defined in several ways. Bachrach and Baratz write that a nondecision "is a decision that results in suppression or thwarting of a latent or manifest challenge to the values or interests of the decision-maker. To be more clearly explicit, nondecision-making is a means by which demands for change in the existing allocation of benefits and privileges in the community can be suffocated before they are even voiced; or kept covert; or killed before they gain access to the relevant decision-making arena; or failing all these things, maimed or destroyed in the decision-implementing stage of the policy process."[4]

Bachrach and Baratz mention different forms of nondecision-making: direct and serious *threats* in order to prevent demands for changes in the established order from entering the political process, *intimidation* of the challenger, *cooptation* of challenging persons or groups, *branding* of the challenger by using symbols like "unpatriotic" or "socialistic," and *burying* the demand in committees.

All these kinds of nondecision-making involve some kind of *subject,* who acts to prevent those issues from being raised and getting through the political process. Not less important is, however, the *structural suppression* of issues; namely, suppression where no decisions are made and no agent of this suppression can be identified.

---

1. William Gamson, "Stable Unrepresentation in American Society," *American Behavioral Scientist,* 12, 1968, p. 19.

2. E. E. Schattschneider, *The Semi-Sovereign People* (New York 1960), p. 71.

3. Helga Maria Hernes, "Kvinners plass i den statsteoretiske tenkningen," *Tidsskrift for samfunnsforskning,* 1980, vol. 21, p. 132–33.

4. Peter Bachrach and Morton Baratz, *Power and Poverty.* (New York, 1970), p. 44

Structural suppression means that by a certain organization of society, including the political system, by certain rules and norms some issues are systematically kept away from the political agenda.[5]

This study is about how issues are suppressed. The concept of non-decision-making refers to one stage of this process of suppression. The methodological question is, how to study the suppression of issues, broadly defined as 1) decisional as well as 2) structural suppression? The first conclusion is that in studying suppression of issues, one should not just look for concrete actions (inside or outside the political institutions). In the research one must also try to understand and reveal the *structures* that form the framework, the setting around the political decision-making and agenda-building.

The second conclusion is that one cannot limit analysis to the political institutions. One has to include the actions and structures of the society at large. One must include in the study what Cobb and Elder have named the pre-political processes:

> . . .pre-political, or at least pre-decisional processes often play the most critical role in determining what issues and alternatives are to be considered by the polity and the probable choices that will be made. What happens in the decision-making councils of the formal institutions of government may do little more than recognize, document, and legalize, if not legitimize, the momentary results of a continuing struggle of forces in the larger social matrix.[6]

To sociologists, socialists, feminists, and others these two conclusions are probably not surprising. Perhaps they are to political scientists. But the question still is, how to translate this approach into tools which can be used in empirical research?

---

5. Bachrach and Baratz may be interpreted as using this broader concept of nondecision-making.

6. Roger W. Cobb and Charles D. Elder, *Participation in American Politics. The Dynamics of Agenda-Building* (Boston, 1972), p. 12.

What are Women's Issues?

> She was a commander—that did not exist—for an army—that did not
> exist—about an idea, which for want of a commander and an army
> probably will never win a clear existence in the understanding of the na-
> tion.[7]

There is no clear concept of "women's issues" or "feminist issues."
That is just the point. For the politicians there have been only a number of mutually independent cases which have something to do with
women—especially legislation which has gender as a criterion. (For
instance, rules that prescribe different treatment of men and women
like the old electoral laws which excluded women, or the new laws of
preferential treatment, or rules which repealed former legal discrimination and thus prescribed formal equality between the sexes.) For
most politicians, women's situation has been dealt with only in small
pieces and often indirectly.

The women's movements, on the other hand, have worked
with every little piece of legislation or measure as an integrated part
of a larger project: that of changing women's position fundamentally.

When I say "women's issues" and not "feminist issues," it is to indicate that I am interested in how public policy in general affects the situation of women, not just policy that *explicitly* affects women. It is
also interesting to study those measures which do not mention gender
explicitly but nevertheless have very different, maybe unnoticed, effects for men and women because of the different social positions of
the sexes—an obvious example of nondecision.

The women's organizations have never agreed upon the goals and
the strategy for changing women's subordinate status. Positions differ
as to whether all women have some common interests regardless of
class differences, and whether women's organizations should work
together. Even the organizations that would call themselves feminist
do not have a common concept of women's interests. Moreover, as

---

7. Said about Mathilde Fibiger, the lonely pioneer of the feminist cause in
Denmark in the 1850s.

everybody knows, not all women want to change the status quo. Feminist ideology is not always translated into proposals ready for the political agenda. The new women's liberation movement especially does not work this way. One of the essential differences between the traditional women's rights organizations and the new women's liberation movement is exactly that the former usually have directed their activity towards public authorities and therefore adjusted their demands to the norms of the recipient, whereas the new women's liberation movement first and foremost addresses women in general.

Cobb and Elder talk about dreams versus claims transformed into what are considered legitimate claims with immediate agenda status. The problem for all deprived groups is that in changing dreams into agendas they risk losing sight of the vision, the utopia. But if they do not do this, they risk having someone else make the agenda for them and distorting the perspective even more.

Feminist organizations have worked hard to make the general public and the politicians see women's position as an issue in its own right rather than as a side of family policy (which in itself is a relatively new set of issues from the 1930s). Politicians, public opinion in general, and many women have denied the existence of a "woman question." To me, this is an example of suppression of issues. To reach this conclusion, I start from the assumption that women are oppressed. To talk about oppression implies a challenge to the belief that women are in their natural position in society. It implies that women's position can and must be changed.

Another assumption is that society is characterized by conflicts, one of which is the conflicting interest of men and women, both in general and within each class. The conflicting interests stem from the fact that women and men have very different positions in the family, in the workplace and in political life, and from the fact that all women are deprived of resources, power and prestige compared to men of their own class.

A Scheme for Studying Agenda-Building which Includes the Aspect of Issue-Suppression

Elaborating on the model made by Bachrach and Baratz, Figure 1 presents a scheme for studying political agenda-building, including the aspect of suppression of issues.[8] The purpose is to study how issues are raised into the political agenda and how they are suppressed. This includes the question of how the barriers are overcome.[9] By looking at the relation women/politics, I hope to be able to throw light on how the political agenda-building process works in relation to a group with few resources, whose values and preferences are not incorporated into the dominant political culture. This interest in the way the political system functions does not imply that the subject of women's issues is merely a case study to me. I am interested in women's issues and the feminist cause as a significant problem in itself.

Figure 1. A scheme for studying political agenda-building

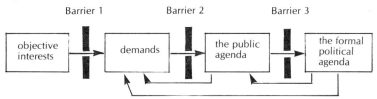

The analysis must include a study of the relevant *structural setting* of the society at large, and of the political system, as well as a study of the concrete *actions* and attitudes.

As an ideal type of agenda-building—in a Weberian sense—a group will begin to realize its objective interests, first individually, then collectively, and form organizations which raise demands. These demands will reach the public agenda (public debate) and later someone will place the issues on the agenda of the formal political institutions (following the straight arrows). I have not included the output and the outcome, since the focus is on agenda-building. But obviously there is feed-back from the outcomes to the objective interests and the de-

8. Bachrach and Baratz, *op.cit.,* p. 54.

9. I have been inspired by Søren Christensen & Poul-Erik Daugaard Jensen, *Magt og deltagelse,* Institute of Organization and Sociology of Work, Copenhagen, 1980; Finn Reske-Nielsen, "Nyere tendenser inden for magtforskningen: Aspekter af begrebet nondecisionmaking," in *Okonomi og Politik,* nr.2,1977; Barbara J. Nelson, "Setting the Public Agenda: The Case of Child Abuse" in May & Wildavsky, *The Policy Cycle* (Sage, 1978).

mands, just as feed-back will occur from the content of the formal political agenda to the public agenda, and from both these agendas to
the demands (curved arrows).

In reality the agenda-building process does not always follow the
route of the ideal type. Some issues may be raised within the political
institutions themselves. Others come from the outside but are stopped
en route. Not all demands will reach the public agenda or the formal
political agenda. The political system is biased and certain issues and
interests are suppressed. This can be expressed in this way: *barriers* or
filters (in the figure represented by vertical spiral lines) systematically
prevent certain issues from being raised and from becoming part of
the political agenda. The concept of nondecision-making, here defined as decisional as well as structural, will in this study be identified
with Barrier 3. Bachrach and Baratz have made the important observa-
tion that while advocates of change must win at all stages of the political process, the defenders of existing policy must win at only one
stage in the process in order to stop the challenge.[10]

This suppression of issues takes place not only through open action
like burying a proposal in a committee (cf. the examples of Bachrach
and Baratz), but also through a certain structural organization of society which favors certain issues and makes barriers for others: The socialization of women, which long prevented us from questioning the
patriarchal order, made a very efficient structural barrier (Barrier 1).
Lack of resources will also prevent a group from raising demands or
from having its demands publicly heard. Also, the structure of the political institutions forms barriers against certain issues and interests.
For example, the fact that certain resources are necessary for one to
become a political representative means that exactly those who have
an interest in challenging the existing distribution of resources do not
have the opportunity to be elected in great numbers. And the system
of corporate interest-representation within the state administration
does in (its well-established Western form) make strong barriers for
those interests that are not integrated into this system (Barrier 3).

If we want to understand the suppression of issues, we must start
from the assumption of *objective interests*. If we do not, we cannot

---

10. Bachrach and Baratz, *op. cit.*, p. 58.

grasp the most important form of issue-suppression, that of preventing issues from being raised at all. As Crenson starts with the assumption that people want to avoid being intoxicated by pollution, so the following case starts with the assumption that women as well as other disenfranchised groups have an objective interest in achieving the right to vote. But there is no reason to try to hide the fact that the question of objective interests is very delicate.

How can one grasp the influence of the *structures* of the whole social setting and of the specific structures of direct relevance, in a study of agenda-building? It is one thing to state that this is a necessary approach; it is yet another thing to do it in practice. For more systematic analysis of the influence of the social structures, a *comparative approach* of some kind seems appropriate. In order to isolate the most important factors of the structural setting that further or hinder certain issues from getting ahead, one could compare the agenda-building of specific issues in different countries or in different historical periods. The case study of women's suffrage in Denmark, below, makes use of the latter approach.

It is the interest in how the *formal political agenda* is ultimately formed that developed the agenda-building approach. The scope of government action is thus a central theme of agenda-building studies. It should, however, be kept in mind that the new women's liberation movement—like some other social movements concerned with reshaping social relations—does not direct its activities mainly toward the state. This is in contrast to the traditional women's rights movement, which has always put much emphasis on influencing public authorities. But even the new feminists have to deal with the formal political institutions on issues like abortion, divorce and equal pay.

From Objective Interests to Demands

The step from interests to demands no doubt involves the biggest hurdle. Women (and other deprived groups as well) have through history been told that their subordinate position is natural. The first step is to challenge this belief, supported though it has been by all authorities: schools, religion, physicians, mothers and fathers. Through heavy socialization with just as heavy sanctions for disobedience, women

41

have been told to be satisfied with their position as the second sex. And if the burden of being the second sex grew too heavy, then women were offered a pedestal.

Only in the case of the militant suffrage movement in England and in a few incidents caused by the new women's liberation movement has it been necessary to use police force to keep women in their "proper" place. Otherwise teachers, parents, magazines and other voices of the establishment have done the job successfully.

I shall not develop this at any length. The literature on socialization of girls and women has grown enormously in recent years. It is, however, worth noting that other ways of preventing interests from being formulated have also been at work; for instance, lack of access to information.

Bachrach and Baratz felt it impossible to make empirical studies of nondecision-making when open conflicts are absent. Such a conclusion severely limits the scope of the concept of issue suppression. In their very interesting study of unemployment as a political issue in American politics, Schlozman and Verba state that in their opinion Bachrach and Baratz yield too much to their critics.[11] Schlozman and Verba themselves have used survey studies to learn why the deprived, in their case the unemployed, do not politicize their needs.

In my study I find it necessary to go further into the question of objective interests. Ultimately, one needs a concept of *women's oppression*[12] in order to talk about women's objective interests, potential needs and false consciousness. But, unlike the Marxian concept of exploitation, which is based on the relation of the classes to the means of production and on the extraction of surplus value, we do not have a clear concept of women's oppression. Still, this concept must be much broader than the concept of exploitation, if only because the op-

---

11. Kay Lehman Schlozman and Sidney Verba, *Injury to Insult. Unemployment, Class, and Political Response* (Cambridge, Mass., 1979), p. 11.

12. Virgina Sapiro has an interesting discussion of the concept of oppression. She used the concept as a social–psychological phenomenon. The concept of oppression I use is broader, covering the structural position of women in society. See Virgina Sapiro, "Sex and Games: On Oppression and Rationality," *British Journal of Political Science*, vol. 9, 1979, pp. 385–408.

pression of women derives from a great spectrum of relations—those within the workplace, the family, and political life.

To come closer to a solution, I think one must thoroughly analyze women's conditions in various spheres and examine the functions that the subordinate position of women has for the structure of the society. One must investigate the unequal distribution of power, resources, prestige, money, property, spare time, etc. within the specific period, country, and class. Then one can start to ask how women have challenged this distribution, or try to illustrate the structures that have prevented women from challenging it.

The step from objective interests to demands involves many aspects. In fact it is two steps. The first is to raise a *subjective* interest: that women individually begin to think that something is wrong. But as in the case of battered wives, women long felt this was just an individual problem. The next step is a *collective consciousness* about the issues and the forming of organizations to raise the demand.

The women's movements have always realized that the first and most serious problem to overcome was to make women realize that they are oppressed. All social movements know of this problem. For women, the very foundation of the first women's movements had a tremendous effect in itself. As Schlozman and Verba state: ". . . Consciousness begets mobilization, but it is undoubtedly the case that mobilization begets consciousness."[13] The new women's liberation movement has from its start emphasized consciousness-raising—not that of the authorities, but that of women.

The Public Agenda

Cobb and Elder distinguish between the *systemic* (or public) agenda and the *formal* (governmental or institutional) agenda. In studying women's issues, I will use the same distinction, slightly altered. The *public agenda*[14] is here defined as all the issues that are given public

---

13. Schlozman and Verba, *op. cit.,* p. 20.

14. The systemic or public agenda is defined this way by Cobb and Elder: "The systemic agenda consists of all issues that are commonly perceived by members of the political community as meriting public attention and as in-

attention (form part of the public debate) in a society. This is, and has to be, a very diffuse concept. The *formal, institutional agenda*[15] is here defined as issues that are up for consideration by authoritative decision-makers, be it in parliament, local councils, the state administration, the courts or public boards. Unlike Cobb and Elder, I will not limit the concept to those issues that are explicitly up for "active and serious consideration" by the political authorities. Studying the agenda-building concerning women's issues, I have found it appropriate to include matters that have just managed to reach the formal agenda, even if they were never seriously considered. It should be noticed that the formal agenda usually will be a part of the public agenda.

We know that there are many routes to the formal political agenda. For an issue to be raised to public debate is one of them. Probably groups and individuals with the smallest amount of resources need the public debate most in order to reach the formal agenda. But the mass media and other agents of the public debate are, conversely, most interested in listening to those groups that are already incorporated into the political decision-making processes.

There are some theories about how an issue reaches the public agenda. But we do not know much about the role the public agenda plays in the formation of the formal agenda, or how it varies with particular issues and particular systems. One thing should be remembered: in the Western countries the fact that the decisions of authorities are subject to public discussion at all is relatively new. In many present systems, such debate still does not exist.

Contrary to Cobb and Elder, I would put more emphasis on the conflict aspect of the formation of the public agenda. The public agenda is not neutral. It is an expression of power to be able to define what is "commonly perceived." In fact, nothing is commonly perceived. But

---

volving matters within the legitimate jurisdiction of existing governmental authority." (*op. cit.*, p. 85.)

15. The formal agenda is by Cobb and Elder defined as "that set of items explicitly up for the active and serious consideration of authoritative decisionmakers" (*op. cit.*, p. 86).

many groups fight to be in the position of formulating the general will. And some are more successful than others.[16]

Suppression of issues from the public agenda is done not only by direct reaction to certain demands. Suppression takes place also through the structures of the public agenda-making. One could start by asking: What are the *institutions* behind the public agenda-making? How are they structured?

The institutions of the public agenda-making are many and their political influence varies greatly. Among them are the mass media, the political organizations in a broad sense, the literature, and public meetings.

One important barrier to women's issues' reaching the public agenda is the fact that women are more or less excluded from the institutions of the public agenda-making. This is an example of *structural suppression*. In the case study that follows, I will show how women were first totally excluded from this arena and how they have later gained some access. The women's movements have recognized and tried to overcome these barriers by such means as creating their own organizations and their own press and insisting on dealing only with female journalists, for example.

The Formal Political Agenda

With growing state intervention, the scope and content of the formal political agenda have changed dramatically. The portion taken up by women's issues has not uniformly increased during the century. As mentioned in the introduction, there have been two waves of legislation concerning women's status and equality between the sexes, one from 1900–1920 and a second which began in the 1970s and continues in the 1980s. This seems to have been the case in the United States and in the northern and central European countries.

Like many scholars, Bachrach and Baratz have studied and discussed the ways in which issues are suppressed from the formal agenda. This nondecision-making takes place when issues are pre-

---

16. A conception of conflicts between classes forms the basis of Jürgen Habermas' concept of "die Bürgerliche Öffentlichkeit."

vented from being considered at all; or are prevented from being seri-ously considered; or are rejected outright; or are radically altered; or, if and when laws are passed, are stopped during the process of imple-mentation. Again, this suppression of issues may be done directly and openly or beneath the surface. It can be done by agents (opponents) or by the structural setting. An analysis of the methods directed to wom-en's issues must include both aspects.

Some of the structural barriers can be mentioned here: The political parties, the large interest organizations, and the formal political insti-tutions are structured around other conflict dimensions. This means that feminist issues, like many other new or not accepted issues, have to create new channels of access. The effort to create a women's politi-cal party made in several countries after the enfranchisement of women was an attempt to introduce new goals and new dimensions into the political system, which was formed before women had the right to participate. These attempts generally have not been success-ful.[17]

The study of agenda-building and issue-suppression as they relate to women's issues raises some interesting questions:

1) What is the influence of women's organizations in the formula-tion of the formal agenda?

Do issues always reach the agenda through pressure from below? Or were many women's issues on the formal agenda generated through other sources? For instance, the Equal Treatment Act (Den-mark, 1978) seems to have come from the EEC authorities.

2) What is the role of the political parties in raising women's issues?

As noted earlier, the political parties in most countries seem to have tried to avoid politicization of the issue of women's position and status. The Swedish political parties are an exception as far as the last two or three elections are concerned. But have the political parties generally been leaders of opinion concerning women's is-sues?

3) What is the role of women's "political elite" (e.g. legislators)?

---

17. Drude Dahlerup, "Women's Entry into Politics: The Experience of the Danish Local and General Elections 1908–20," *Scandinavian Political Stud-ies*, new series, vol. 1, nos. 2–3, pp. 138–62.

Studies of the role of the few women political representatives have often shown a picture of tokenism and cooptation. Recent research seems, however, to indicate that even if women legislators have not been feminists they have nevertheless played an important role in raising women's issues to the formal political agenda.[18]

4) What is the relation between the women's movement, women political elites, and political parties?

Even that part of the women's movement which does not want to get involved with political authorities probably has some impact on the formal agenda. The existence of strong women's movements outside the political institutions seems to be a prerequisite for the influence of the women political elite inside the system. In general, one may assume that the impact of the women's movement is strongest in the first stages of issue-raising. Later the issues are left to (and altered by) the women in the formal political institutions.

A Case Study: How the Issue of Women's Suffrage Was Raised in Danish Politics

The history of women's suffrage in Denmark falls into four periods: 1849–1867, 1868–1900, 1901–1918, and after 1918. The analysis must examine the general social and political structure of the periods as well as the specific actions, perceptions and arguments concerning votes for women. The historical approach comparing different periods leads to a discussion of how the general social and political setting influenced the possibilities of raising the issue. What follows is a compressed analysis of the history of women's suffrage in Denmark. The question of a general bias of the political system against women's issues cannot be analyzed on the basis of one case only. It would take a broad selection of cases and an overall view of policy outcomes to study the *gender-specific* selectivity of the political system, a term bor-

---

18. See Sirkka Sinkkonen and Elina Haavio-Manilla, "The Impact of the Women's Movement and Legislative activity of the Women MPs on Social Development," in Margherita Rendel (ed), *Women, Power and Political Systems* (London, 1981).

rowed from Claus Offe, who talks about the *class-specific* selectivity of the political systems.[19]

First Period: 1849–1867

En resumé: –No demands for women's suffrage were raised by women—or men

–no public debate about women's suffrage

–Women's suffrage never reached the formal political agenda. It was out of the question.

When the liberal, democratic constitutions were established in Europe and the United States, women's right to participate in political life was generally not discussed at all. It was simply not an issue. The process, which was supposed to transform subjects into citizens did not involve women, nor all men. The citizen was assumed to be a white, male, adult property-owner or at least head of his own household (which included women, children and servants). The first liberal constitution in Denmark was introduced in 1849, enfranchising all men with a household of their own, provided they did not receive help under the Poor Law, a relatively broad franchise.

I find no problems in claiming that women—as well as other disenfranchised groups—had an *objective* interest in getting the vote, namely in order to take care of their own interests, even if voting would never solve all their problems. From this starting point the first period mentioned here can be characterized as a period in which the issue of women's suffrage was suppressed from the political agenda in Denmark, and prevented from even being raised—not by direct action, but by the whole social setting.

In general, women did not challenge this setting. Tremendous ideological pressure was telling them that they were placed where God and Nature had intended them to be: in a subordinate position as the assistant to husband or father. (That women's "proper place" varied from class to class did not seem to bother the ideologists.) The fundamental changes that industrialization made in women's (and men's)

---

19. Claus Offe, *Strukturprobleme des kapitalistischen Staates* (Suhrkamp Verlag, 1977).

condition did not to any great extent reach women until later in the century. In general, women lacked resources, possibilities, and the necessary insurgent imagination to revolt. During this period no collective action was made by women, and no women's organizations were formed. Only two or three isolated women openly challenged the traditional view of women's proper place, using fiction as their medium. But we know from memoirs that some of the better educated Danish women were very much influenced by the national and constitutional debate of the time and knew about "women's emancipation" as something discussed abroad. Although women's suffrage was not on the *general public agenda,* a first debate concerning what was called the "woman question" took place in the 1850s. This debate was sparked by a book written under the nom-de-plume of Clara Raphael by a 19-year-old governess, Mathilde Fibiger, who was patronized by Johan Ludvig Heiberg, one of the leaders of the literary circles in Denmark. The debate, which died shortly, did not deal with political rights for women but solely with women's right to individual freedom and intellectual development.

The structures which carried the "public debate" in this period generally excluded women. During the period of censorship (1799–1848, de facto until the 1830s), the public political debate took place mostly through books, plays and literary magazines, and as already mentioned the few women who raised the "woman question" did so through fiction. Even so, they were met with strong reaction, since women were not supposed to raise their voices in public. Women were expected to remain socially invisible.

In the 1830s, political associations and clubs began to emerge, but again women were usually excluded from this form of public discussion. In fact, one could say that the relative situation of women from the newly political active classes, i.e. the bourgeois and the intellectuals in the cities and the landlords and independent farmers in the countryside, was harmed by this new public arena. Until then, political discussion had taken place in the home, a place where women could participate or at least listen. Public discussion in a public arena, where women were not supposed to appear, reinforced women's political exclusion. In the same way, the new constitution in fact introduced a dividing line between men and women.

49

The establishment of a new forum for public debate, which emerged as a link between the private sphere and the state, gave no room to women. During this period women usually did not even participate in public celebrations. The first woman who tried to mount a platform, Mathilde Fibiger, was removed by force. Not until 1865 did a woman speak from a public platform. Thus, the structure of the public sphere itself did not invite women to participate, and the participating men did not by themselves take up women's issues.

The question of votes for women as well as other aspects of women's condition did *not* reach the *formal political agenda* in the political institutions of that time. And it is unnecessary to say that the rules of these institutions barred women from participating. It was men who could "give" women the vote. This fact meant that the later women's movement in fighting for the vote always had to try to be accepted as an organization respected by men and operating on the premises of men.

When the first "free" constitution (1849) was written and discussed in Denmark, women's suffrage was simply not a part of the debate. No one argued against votes for women. No one had to. This is a most clear example of tacit nondecision-making based on the ruling elite's consensus that women's place was at home. In the constitutional assembly, one of the participants, a university professor, merely mentioned as an unquestioned fact:

> It is universally acknowledged that minors, children, womenfolk and criminals should not have the franchise.

A Short Note on Other Countries

The history of the enfranchisement of women shows striking similarities among the Western countries. In all of them women were slow to challenge the liberal notion that the concept of the dignity of the individual and the axiom that all men were born equal and had the right to self-government applied only to men. Teresa Brennan and Carole Pateman have shown that the "free individual" of the liberal ideology was in fact only the male head of the household. Women, and especially married women, caused liberal authors much trouble.[20] Helga Maria Hernes has also shown that in the liberal and continental theories of the state and the citizen, the political individual was, indeed, of male sex.[21] Rodney Barker argues that women's exclusion from the suffrage was not discussed by the early constitutionalists because only male heads of families were considered individuals and citizens:

> The characteristic of the prevailing conception of citizenship was not that it involved limitation by age and sex, but rather that it was given meaning by a series of specific and unquestioned assumptions about the social and economic character of the essential person. This person was taken to be male and adult, and insofar as this was not the case, then something less than a normal person was involved. This was not a matter of political preferences or values so much as of how the political world was seen.[22]

> This world was viewed with a perception of the normal member which excluded the majority of people. The smallest political unit was taken to be not the individual, nor even the person over the age of twenty-one, but the adult male, with a subordinate and supporting family which constituted his private hinterland, was personal to him, and was cut off from the rest of society by him.[23]

This tacit exclusion of women from citizenship and hence from voting rights was seen in many countries.

The Danish constitution of 1849 did mention that the franchise was limited to males over a certain age with independent households of

---

20. Teresa Brennan and Carole Pateman, "Mere Auxiliaries to the Commonwealth: Women and the Origins of Liberalism," *Political Studies,* vol. XXVII, no. 2, June 1979, p. 183ff. They also claim that the social changes of that time, contrary to what is generally believed, in fact strengthened patriarchy.

21. Helga Maria Hernes, *op. cit.*

22. I would not hold people's perception of reality as something distinct from their political preferences and values. One's perception of reality does structure one's values, and vice versa.

23. Rodney Barker, *Political Ideas in Modern Britain* (London, 1978), p. 113.

their own. But in some earlier constitutions and constitutional declarations, the exclusion of women was not made explicitly. The American Declaration of 1776 talks about the inalienable rights of all men. This could mean both males and all human beings, but the founding fathers undoubtedly referred only to white males. In the same way, the French Declaration of Human Rights from 1789 did not find it necessary to state explicitly that these rights were valid for males only. In England, it was not until the electoral law of 1832 (which extended the suffrage to a larger, if still small, number of males) that it was explicitly stated that women did not have the right to vote. It is known that in some countries, for instance in France and England, a few women have long had some kind of political rights. These rights belonged to them not as women, however, but as property owners, such as widowed noblewomen.

Women could "without inconvenience" be excluded from political rights, James Mill wrote in the *Encyclopaedia Britannica* in 1824, because their interests were included in those of their fathers or their husbands. So it was conceived by the politicians well into the 20th century. But some men and women challenged this concept; e.g., William Thompson in his book *Appeal of One Half the Human Race,* 1825, which was a furious answer to James Mill: So did Olympe de Gouges and the political clubs for women during the French Revolution; and Abigail Adams during the American Revolution.[24]

Demand for the vote, however, was not usually the first demand women made as they began to challenge the patriarchal society. In cases of national or revolutionary upheaval, the claim for enfranchisement came early because women had experienced exclusion because of sex when they wanted to participate in the uprisings. Generally the demand for the vote came after a broader discussion of the whole "woman question" had begun. Even Mary Wollstonecraft mentioned the question of political representation for women only in a single cautious sentence in her famous book in 1792. Women ought to have their own political representatives, she said, "even if this proposal probably will cause laughter." In short, women had to be acknowledged—by themselves and by some men at least—as human beings,

---

24. Drude Dahlerup, *Socialisme og kvindefrigørelse i det 19. århundrede.* 1973. (Socialism and women's emancipation in the 19th century).

as individuals, before the demand for suffrage could be raised. It was a case of suppression of issues, not by any agent, but by the entire social setting.

Second Period: 1868–1900

En resumé: –Women began to organize, and some women's organizations, but not all, raised the question of women's suffrage.

–The enfranchisement of women now entered the public agenda, but it was not given much attention and reactions were mostly negative.

–Women's suffrage reached the formal political agenda but was repeatedly buried in committee or simply rejected.

During this period, the issue of women's suffrage moved from total silence into the public debate and the formal political agenda, but it was not accepted. The period was characterized by large social changes. In Denmark it was a period when industrialization began to speed up, the working class was constituted, and fundamental changes occurred in women's conditions: women in the countryside lost much of their former employment because commodities were now produced by industry. Together with a growing population surplus, this forced many women to move to the towns, where they became domestic servants or factory girls. When married, working-class women often had to work long hours outside the home in hard and low-paying jobs. The unmarried women from the middle classes and the intelligentsia could no longer find employment or occupation within the families and therefore wanted to break the male monopoly on higher education and suitable jobs. Married women from these classes lived in diminishing households and were either "reduced" to housewives with only one or no maidservant or, if rich, became superfluous.

During this period, the political parties were established, and organizations emerged everywhere. Collective tensions were growing between the classes, and for a long period, in the 1880s, the Danish parliament was paralyzed by a conflict over the constitution and over the national defense between the Conservatives and the Agrarian-

Liberals. It was within this framework that some women tried to raise the question of suffrage.

Women now began to organize, but in small numbers only. In 1871, the first women's rights organization in Denmark, the Danish Women's Society (Dansk Kvindesamfund) emerged and still exists. Its program was very similar to those of the women's rights movement all over Europe and in the United States. But the Danish organization did not place the suffrage on its program until 1906. That demand was considered too radical and too dangerous. Partly because of the reluctance of the Danish Women's Society on the voting issue, several other women's organizations were formed in the 1880s, e.g. the Women's Union for Progress (Kvindelig Fremskridtsforening), 1885. These new organizations openly claimed and worked for the vote through large public meetings, petitions to parliament, interpellations to candidates, etc. Thus, in the 1880s women collectively raised the issue of votes for women, but resistance in parliament and the whole political conflict of the period, discouraged the women's organizations, and most of them were dissolved around 1890.

The Danish Women's Society always stressed that it was a *"nonpolitical" organization* that worked in the interest of *all women*. This approach almost paralyzed the organization during the constitutional conflict of the 1880s, which divided the political scene. Since the left showed a more positive (although not enthusiastic) attitude towards women's suffrage, and the Conservatives were definitely against, then a demand for votes for women would be accused of being "political." This has been a dilemma for the Danish Women's Society throughout history.

In the 1870s and 80s, working-class women began to organize as well, in trade unions and to a very small extent within the Social Democratic party, which was started in 1871. But again, the number of organized women before the turn of the century remained very small. Working-class women and women socialists did not join the women's rights organizations, which they rightly regarded as upper-middle-class organizations. During this period, some of the trade unions for women workers began, however, to cooperate with the women's rights organizations on the suffrage issue.

It should be mentioned that the very idea that women should organize met with resistance within the male section of the labor movement and within other circles of the society. From all Western countries, we know the means that were used in order to keep women from getting together and making themselves socially visible outside their homes. In public debate, these women were accused of being man-hating spinsters, of being mannish and frustrated. In their homes they were prevented from participation either by their husbands or by the threat of the practical problems they would face if they left.

When working-class women began to demand a place for themselves and their interests within the labor movement, they were met with the accusation that women's claims were splitting up the working class. This was a very serious accusation, involving the whole discussion of sex versus class. In short, my point of view is that the working class was in fact already split up, namely into men and women. When the leaders stressed the common interests of working-class men and women (which they did), they neglected the conflicts between men and women within the working class—conflicts which sprang from their very different positions at home, at the workplace and in political life.[25]

Women's suffrage was now openly discussed in public—had reached the *public agenda*—but the issue was not given much attention.

The structure which carried the public debate changed a great deal during this period. The formation of large political organizations—interest organizations, political parties and trade unions, for example—established new arenas for public political discussions. The literature, which was mostly inter-Scandinavian, still had a very strong position in the formation of public opinion.[26] But the literature soon met competition from the growing number of newspapers that were circulated in much larger numbers than even the works of the leading au-

---

25. Drude Dahlerup, "Hvilken klasse tilhorer kvinden? Hvilket kon har arbejderen?" (Of which class is woman? Of which sex is the worker?), in *Forum for kvindeforskning,* vol. 1, no. 2, 1981.

26. Pil Dahlerup, "Kvindebevaegelsen og litteraturen" in Inga Dahlsgaard (ed.), *Kvindebevaegelsens Hvem-Hvad-Hvor,* 1975, pp. 145–177.

thors.[27] In general, however, the number of people who "counted" and who participated in the public debate of those days was much lower than today.

The arenas of public discussion were still dominated by men. But during this period, women began to challenge the ideology that kept them out of public life. The formation of women's organizations can be regarded as a way of creating room for women in the public debate, since women were still excluded formally or by convention from most political parties and other new organizations. Women organized independently because men excluded them and because it was still rather unthinkable that women should sit at meetings side by side with men. But the women's autonomous organizations and the few women's sections within male organizations also gave women a place where they, for the first time, could try to formulate what their interests were, what they wanted.

During this period women began to make public speeches and to attend meetings. But the reaction was still quite strong. Also during this period, women became visible in the previously all-male positions of teacher in public schools (since 1859), university student (since 1875), union leader, doctor (the first, 1885), and last but not least, writer. Women began to write—even though the ordinary history of literature has managed to overlook them until recently. In their fiction and poetry, female authors expressed critiques of the patriarchal family. They met with strong reaction, and the critics (composed of the male literary establishment) were often very harsh to their works.

From the 1870s the "woman question" was on the public agenda first and foremost through literature, and it was intensively discussed by female as well as male authors. In the 1880s the great Nordic debate about chastity appeared; it was called the "Chastity Controversy." The participants were female authors and many of the most famous men of letters; e.g. Bjørnstjerne Bjørnson, Henrik Ibsen, Georg and Edward Brandes, and August Strindberg.

---

27. Pil Dahlerup mentions that one of the books of the leading author of those days, *Georg Brandes,* was published in 1250 copies, while "Politiken," one of the new newspapers (1884), reached 4,000 subscribers in half a year. *op. cit.,* p. 148.

What about women's suffrage? The debate about the whole "woman question" no doubt constituted the basis that made the demand for suffrage possible. But the public debate did not deal much with suffrage. The women's organizations with suffrage on their programs did try hard to make this an important issue, but they failed. The female authors usually dealt with the problems of women in marriage and the home sphere, not directly with the vote.

Women's organizations soon made their own journals. This was a way of breaking through the male monopoly of the public debate and of making women's voices heard. In 1885, the journal of the Danish Women's Society, Kvinden og Samfundet, appeared. In 1888, Women's Union for Progress published the first issue of its journal, called "What-We-Want. The Journal of Feminism, Peace and Labour." This journal demanded votes for women.

Further, the debate about the suffrage was raised by John Stuart Mill's famous essay, *The Subjection of Women,* which was translated into Danish the very year it was issued in England, 1869. It was translated by Georg Brandes who in his introduction supported the claim that women should have the right to participate in political life. In a later edition, however, he withdrew this support. He then claimed that women's suffrage had to wait, because he feared that it would strengthen the religious-political reaction.

During this period, suffrage for women reached the *formal political agenda* in Denmark for the first time, together with other issues concerning women's status; e.g. a Married Women's Property Act passed in 1880. In all Western countries, the suffrage was never the first women's issue to succeed. Legislation, which gave first unmarried, then married women legal majority, always came before the vote. In Denmark, quite a few proposals concerning women's positions were presented in parliament in the 1880s, but partly because of the political fight almost nothing was passed.

How was the issue of women's suffrage raised in the political institutions? Not by the political parties. The parties were, as mentioned above, formed as Conservatives, Agrarian-Liberals, and Social Democrats. The parties were formed on the basis of social conflicts which did not at all include any woman question. To raise a woman question across the party lines, as the Danish Women's Society tried to do, was almost impossible. But it was almost as impossible to get women's problems on the agenda *within* each political party. Women's suffrage, like other women's issues, was not taken up as an issue between the political parties. Every politician reacted in a personal way to this question. It was never part of party politics. To those women who tried to raise the question, it was a kind of nondecision-making that was very hard to overcome.

In the late 1860s, the Danish parliament for the very first time discussed suffrage for women, namely as a minor problem in a debate on establishing parish councils. In 1868 widows who were heads of households were granted the right to decide over church affairs as members of the "Free Churches." For the next several years (until the issue was resolved in 1903), parliament discussed proposals by the opposition to establish parish councils within the state church, and in this connection it had its first—uncertain—debates on women's suffrage. Debate began by treating suffrage as a privilege of property owners, but slowly suffrage came to be treated as a right of the individual. This was important for women, and in this way the question of souls before God and God's church seems to have furthered the individualistic view. Thus no public debate took place concerning women's participation in church affairs. It was only a minor problem in another discussion. Not until the 1880s did suffrage for women enter the agenda of the Danish parliament as a question in itself.

In 1886 the first bill proposing municipal votes for women was presented to parliament by Frederik Bajer who, together with his wife, was a leading member of the Danish Women's Society. But he did so without the consent of the society, since they did not have women's suffrage on their program. After that bills concerning votes for women were presented to parliament many times. They were met with the more open kind of nondecision-making: they were buried in a committee or were passed by the lower house but rejected by the upper house. The resistance caused Bajer to limit his proposal to votes for a small number of women only, excluding married women among others. This concession did not help; in fact it split women supporters.

The parliamentary debates can be studied in order to find out the tactics used to keep this issue from being passed or, at times, from even being considered. The arguments were the same as in most countries and need not be repeated here. They ran from emotional speeches about women's proper place and the probable end of marriage to sheer suppression. The best example of the latter was a resolution by means of which the upper house repeatedly rejected requests to discuss women's suffrage: "Being convinced that the enfranchisement of women would be in the interest of neither themselves nor of the society at large, the Upper House will proceed to the next business."

The way the suffrage bills were treated in parliament as well as in the whole political setting during the period affected not only the strategy, but also the very programs of the women's organizations. One example of this is the simple fact that the Danish Women's Society did not have suffrage on their program. It is rather easy to see this as a suppression of issues, since we know that many individuals in the organization did want the vote and as individuals did work for the cause. In 1887 they forced the organization to adopt the demand for suffrage for the first time. But this created such a fuss in "public opinion" that an extraordinary general meeting was summoned and the dangerous demand was again removed from the program—for the next 20 years.

Third Period: 1901–1915

En resumé: —mass mobilization of women around the demand for the vote

—the enfranchisement of women on the public agenda more and more as something that had to come some day

—women's suffrage on the formal political agenda, but always combined with other issues. During this period, Danish women won the right to vote, step by step.

Generally, this period was a time of reform. The Agrarian-Liberals came to power in 1901 and had started a large reform program. The landlords lost their political and social power. The class-war was being institutionalized in the political arena and on the labor market.

During this period, women became organized on a mass basis in

59

the labor market. Women's voluntary associations flourished. In general, many women now became organized for various purposes.

Women made their entry into the political parties especially after women got the right to vote in local elections (1908). This event made the parties suddenly interested in women. In 1915, women made up 16.9 percent of the members of the Social Democratic party.[28] In Denmark, women did not (were not allowed to) form women's sections within the parties until the 1930s which, compared to other European countries, was very late.[29]

During these years, women entered the jobs of the middle layer in great numbers. Formal barriers to women's entry into education and jobs were removed step by step. Women entered the public sector, but not without resistance from the men who feared the competition of cheaper female labor. Women of the working class were still mostly domestic servants or industrial workers, if unmarried. And hard-working homeworkers, if married, often performed additional low-paid work for others in the home or outside the home. In the countryside, women were still the assistants of their husbands. If unmarried, they were servant girls.

Women now demanded the vote in a larger number than ever before. The Danish Women's Society in 1906 formally included the demand in its program. The society, which had no more than 1,000 members in the decades before the turn of the century, had 7,000 in 1910.

Especially when the *local* vote was won, women from various sections of society united in the struggle for the vote. Several organizations were established especially to fight for the vote, while organizations formed around other purposes also joined the struggle. Political

---

28. Drude Dahlerup, "Udviklingslinier i kvinders politiske deltagelse og repraesentation i Danmark", i Mogens N. Pedersen (ed.), *Dansk Politik i 1970'erne*, 1979, pp. 111–150, here p. 121. Information about women's part of the party membership are not available for other parties.

29. Drude Dahlerup, *The Women's Sections within the Political Parties in Denmark. Their history, function, and importance—for the political parties, for women, and for feminism.* Paper presented to the ECPR conference, Grenoble, 1978.

and social divisions split up women in various organizations, but they did what the great leader of the German socialist women's movement, Clara Zetkin, had asked: "getrennt marschierend, vereinigt schlagend" (marching separately, but fighting together). Women united in fighting for the vote as *a goal in itself,* even if they did not agree upon what the vote should be used for once it was won. The situation after the enfranchisement revealed this disagreement.[30]

In Denmark, the fight for the vote was never as militant as in England. But the violent events in England were very well known in Denmark, and the respectable Danish women's organizations used the English experiences as a threat and as a proof of their own respectability.

Women's emancipation was now a part of the *public agenda,* but again it never constituted a major issue, except in the journals of the women's organizations. And those were designed especially as a means to force women's issues to public concern. Votes for women was also discussed, but more and more it turned into an issue which people thought would soon be solved. The opponents only hoped to be able to postpone it for as long as possible.

During this period women began to get voting rights in other countries, and the Danish women's organizations took care that every victory abroad was made publicly known. There is no doubt that it supported the opinion that the enfranchisement *had to* come some day. It seems that this opinion in some ways prevented further discussion and made it difficult for the women's organizations to mobilize public opinion on the matter.

Still there were many opponents to the vote and to women's emancipation in general. But whereas opponents earlier could make the most uninformed and contemptuous remarks about women and nobody would react, women now had the resources and the power to answer.

Women still used literature as a medium to express their opinions, but in general, the role of literature as a force in the creation of public opinion was diminishing. Newspapers, magazines, and light literature

---

30. Drude Dahlerup, *op. cit., Scandinavian Political Studies,* new series, vol. 1, nos. 2–3, 1978, pp. 139–62.

were flourishing. And there was a growing split between feminist journals and women's or ladies' magazines. The ideological message of these new magazines was women as consumers and housewives.

During this period, many laws and administrative measures were passed which gave women formal (but not real) equality with men. The "woman question" was on *the formal political agenda*.

Women gradually gained the right to vote. In 1903, women, along with men, got the right to vote and be elected to the new parish councils. This was the first introduction of universal suffrage in Denmark. In the original proposal, domestic servants were excluded from the vote, but the newly formed union of domestic servants (all women) intervened successfully. In 1907, women were enfranchised and became eligible for membership on the new Social Aid Boards. In 1908, more than twenty years after the first bill was proposed, women gained the vote to the local councils and in 1915 to parliament. In all cases, women's suffrage was not the only issue at stake, but was combined with—and concealed by, the women's organizations said—other issues.

The new constitution, which involved universal suffrage, was long delayed, thanks to many other conflicts than the enfranchisement of women. After women had gained the vote in local elections, their parliamentary enfranchisement was almost never subject to discussion. The Danish Women's Society asked that the extension of the suffrage be made into a separate constitutional amendment. In this way, women's suffrage would not be mixed up with and consequently delayed by other conflicts. And in this way, women would get the opportunity to have a say about the other constitutional changes. The demand was rejected. This was not the first time and would definitely not be the last time that an issue concerning women's position was mixed with and *subordinated to other political issues*. In my opinion, this is another kind of nondecision or suppression of issues.

How did the enfranchisement of women reach the formal political agenda? Was it by intervention of the women's organizations? It is worth noticing that in the first instance of voting rights, namely to the parish councils, *no* women's organizations had asked for the vote to these special organs. During the readings, the union of domestic servants intervened for their members. The women's rights organizations often forgot that the servants (their servants!) were women as well. But the initiative originally came from the government. This was also the case concerning the Social Aid Boards. Women's demands for local and parliamentary suffrage had, of course, an indirect impact on these cases.

During this period, the women's organizations for the first time gained *direct access* to the political elites. The Danish Women's Society now went directly to the ministers and the administration with their claims. The organization itself made the drafts of bills concerning women's affairs, sometimes by request from the government. When the leading women's organizations celebrated jubilees and the like, the leading politicians from the Agrarian-Liberals and the Radical-Liberals would be present. The direct access of the Danish Women's Society to the political elites was caused by their shared political attitudes, but also by the growing power of women and women's organizations.

Gunnar Qvist has concluded that the reforms concerning women's position in Sweden from 1809–1920 came mostly because they were in the interest of the male society. They were a part of the political battle between social classes of men.[31] I agree that the answer to *why* women got the vote must be searched for in the social conflicts of society at large as well as in the changing positions of women, which, however, in itself forms a part of the social conflicts of society at large. But I would not go so far as to deny women's organizations any influence on the outcome. I do think, however, that any complete study of *why* women's issues have been rejected or have been passed (perhaps in another form than the women's organizations wanted) must include an analysis of the conflicting interests concerning the specific issue and other issues involved. I have not done that here since my chief concern has been *how* the issue has been raised or been prevented from being raised.

31. Gunnar Qvist, "Et perspektiv på den s.k. kvinnoemancipationen" *(Historisk Tidskrift)*, Sweden 1977, no. 2, pp. 145–180.

Fourth Period: 1918–

After their enfranchisement, no proposals to disenfranchise women were placed before parliament. The issue was no longer on the agenda. The public debate about whether women should have the franchise also stopped and was replaced by a discussion of how women used the vote (usually male discussants) or what the vote should be used for (usually female discussants). No one dared raise his voice to suggest that women should be disenfranchised. We can call this a *creation of new barriers*. It is another kind of hidden suppression of issues. New norms were created which prohibited these issues from being raised again, even though many conservatives still felt that the enfranchisement of women and of servants of both sexes was wrong. The same thing happened to most other extensions of the suffrage: they could not be withdrawn. Now barriers were established which *prevented* opponents of universal suffrage from raising the issue. Those barriers, like the earlier reverse ones, consisted of norms, another structuring of the public debate and the political institutions, now including women participants and a growing power for women as a group and for the nonconservative forces in society.

I am not saying that any issue once solved or settled will never return. That depends upon the nature of the issue and the power of the interests behind it. In the case of suffrage, the changing social position of women—which took place not primarily as a result of public decisions—made it rather impossible for this right to be withdrawn. But fundamental changes in the social and political powers, as the Third Reich has shown, could threaten feminist gains.

Suffrage was only one of the feminist issues. In all Western countries, the women's rights organizations had put so much emphasis on it, however, that they were relatively unprepared as to how to use the vote once it was won. On the other hand, Socialist women did not usually doubt that the vote was a means rather than a goal in itself.

Once women had suffrage, some people concluded that all feminist problems were solved. This was an effort of issue suppression which has hit women's organizations through all the years until the 1970s. The former prime minister of Denmark, I. D. Christensen, declared that once women had been enfranchised, all feminist organizations should be dissolved. Some women's organizations agreed and closed down. One leader said that the feminist cause, after being an isolated issue, an issue in itself, would have to be incorporated into other social issues, the solving of which would contribute to the common good. Other women's organizations, among them the Danish Women's Society, continued to try to raise feminist issues to public concern. But during the inter-war period feminism had a hard time, and many of its forces were being incorporated or swallowed up by the political parties.

Concluding Remarks

This scheme for studying agenda-building can easily be used with other issues as well. It is merely a checklist, showing the stages one should include in order to understand how issues are kept from the political agenda and how barriers are overcome. I admit that the issue of women's suffrage was in a way an "easy" issue to handle because:
1) It is a case which, after the initial silence, was later raised by women and women's movements. This fact makes it easier to ask the question why it was not raised before. Some questions are never raised and consequently involve the analysis of the objective-interests stage more directly.
2) It is a case which was successful in the end. Other issues are never solved nor settled by the political authorities. But exactly this shift from silent suppression to actual settlement allows a comparative analysis of the influence of the (changing) social setting on agenda-making.

The approach used in this study is based on the assumption that the composition of the political agenda and the fate of various issues cannot be understood if the analysis is limited to *decisions* and *actions*. It must include the social and political setting of a given society as well. The approach does make an analysis more comprehensive and time consuming, but reality is complex, even if the rigid boundaries of academic disciplines try to conceal the fact.

One case study, such as the one presented here, cannot give any conclusions about the gender-specific selectivity of the political systems of the Western world. Or phrased differently, whether and to what degree the state is a patriarchal state. What is needed is a broad selection of case studies and overall views of policy outcomes and political processes. In my opinion, our theoretical discussions of the selectivity of the political system in terms of class, race and sex require at this point empirical case studies.

4
THE SHAME OF THE
MARRIAGE CONTRACT

Carole Pateman
University of Sydney
Sydney, Australia

The Shame of the
Marriage Contract
Carole Pateman

The language of contract and contractarian arguments are presently
enjoying a new lease on popular and academic life, as illustrated by
the political success of the libertarian New Right and the academic
success of theoretical works by Rawls and Nozick. The widespread
appeal of contractarian ideas suggests that the "movement from status
to contract" regarded by Sir Henry Maine as the essence of the development of the modern, liberal world, is reaching its practical and theoretical conclusion. It has recently been argued that radical contractarianism is the ideology of our society,[1] but discussions of contract
and the movement from the old world of status rarely extend to the
one contract into which almost everyone enters during her/his life and
which is of great significance for individuals' everyday lives—namely,
the marriage contract. There is, however, a long history of feminist
criticism of the marriage contract, which has been renewed with the
revival of the organized feminist movement, and the recent innovation
of "contract marriage" (in which the two parties freely negotiate the
terms and duration of the written contract which will govern their
lives together) provides another good example of the current popular-
ity of contractarian ideas and practices.[2] The character and strength of

1. D. Gauthier, "The Social Contract as Ideology," *Philosophy and Public
Affairs,* 6,2, 1977, pp. 130–164.

2. On contract marriage see, e.g., L. Weitzman, "Legal Regulation of Marriage: Tradition and Change," *California Law Review,* 62, 1974, pp.
1249–78.

contractarianism as ideology is perhaps better revealed by an analysis of the marriage contract than the more familiar topics of discussion. My argument has something to say about this aspect of the marriage contract but, more importantly, it is concerned with the question whether marriage is essentially contractual. The question was posed in political theory by Hegel, but it is also central to two centuries of feminist debate and struggle about marriage and the marriage contract and to the problem of the alternative form of personal and sexual relationships to be supported by feminists.

In political theory, the movement from status to contract is exemplified in the development of the great conception of the social contract and the claim that the state has (or is as if it has) its origin in a contract. In the seventeenth century discussions of the social contract and the marriage contract went hand in hand, and the similarities and differences between domestic and political order were used to support competing claims about the justified exercise of authority.[3] This candor (and level of understanding) has long since vanished and the marriage contract has been excluded from the mainstream of contemporary theoretical argument. For example, the response to John Stuart Mill's critique of the marriage contract in almost all recent standard commentaries on his work has been to ignore this part of his social and political theory. The neglect is the more striking because the basis of Mill's argument is that liberal principles, including contract, should be extended to marriage. In *The Subjection of Women* he argues that the law governing marriage is "a monstrous contradiction to all the principles of the modern world," and that the social subordination of women is "a single relic of an old world of thought and practice exploded in everything else"[4]—a relic, that is, of the old world of status. A major theme in feminist criticism (but not the only theme as I shall

---

3. M. Shanley, "Marriage Contract and Social Contract in Seventeenth Century English Political Thought," *Western Political Quarterly*, XXXII, 1, pp. 79–91.

4. J.S. Mill, "The Subjection of Women," in J.S. Mill and H. Taylor, *Essays on Sex Equality*, (ed.), A. Rossi (University of Chicago Press, 1970), p. 217; p. 146.

emphasize later) is that the subjection of wives is bound up with the fact that the marriage contract has never been a true contract. Much past and present feminist writing thus seems to point to the conclusion that marriage properly should be contractual. In this respect, feminism contributes to the social pressures aiding the completion of the long movement from status to contract.

There has, of course, always been opposition to contractual conceptions and arguments in political theory, but criticism has concentrated on social contract doctrine. Hegel is one of the greatest of the critics of the social contract, and he is also virtually alone in opposing the contractual conception of marriage. In paragraph 75 of the *Philosophy of Right* he declares that "shameful" is the only word to describe an essentially contractual conception of marriage. Hegel's claim about marriage is rarely discussed. The lack of attention reflects the general neglect of arguments about conjugal relations and domestic life in the work of the classic theorists, but it also arises from a consensus that marriage, as a contractual relation, is unproblematic. On the contrary, almost everything about the marriage contract is questionable—even its existence.

Hegel has good reason to argue that a purely contractual conception of marriage is shameful. He provides the theoretical basis for a critique of present attempts to put contractarianism into practice in personal relations between the sexes, but although Hegel offers a profound philosophical and sociological critique of contractual conceptions and practices he sees only one side of the shame of the marriage contract. Indeed, he endorses the other aspect of its shamefulness which feminists have always tried to bring out into the open: that the position of "wife" in the structure of the institution of marriage is one of ascribed patriarchal subjection or status. What is less clear in feminist arguments is the form of relationship that should replace this shameful status. It is easy to suppose that the problem is resolved if a (potential) wife and husband are able freely to negotiate, as equals, the terms of their marriage contract; the solution appears to lie in an extension of the movement from status to contract to marriage. But the elimination of this last and most deeply entrenched form of status then leads straight into the shame of a contractual conception of marriage.

71

This, too, should concern feminists. If some important feminist arguments follow the logic of the movement from status to contract, wider feminist values and ideals and the vision of a feminist social order stand opposed to contractarianism. Feminists are right to reject Hegel's attempt to give a philosophical justification to the shame of patriarchal subjection in marriage, but they also should applaud his rejection of the shame of contractual marriage.

Feminist Critiques of the Marriage Contract

In 1825, William Thompson laid the foundation for much subsequent feminist criticism of the marriage contract in his *Appeal of One Half The Human Race*. One of Thompson's central arguments is that it is an "audacious falsehood" to talk of a marriage contract. The so-called marriage contract lacks two vital elements of a proper contract and, Thompson argues, the deficiency means that marriage, far from being a contract, is really "the white slave code." A slave is an individual "whose actions and earnings . . . are under the arbitrary control of another human being,"[5] and this, he argues, is an exact description of a wife. A "contract" entails that two parties, of equal standing, voluntarily agree to enter it, but women are forced to marry just as slaves are forced into slavery. In reply to the obvious objection that, unlike slaves, women have a choice because they can remain single, Thompson argues that social custom and law (made by men) effectively deprive women of the means to earn their living, so that unless they give up hope of a decent life they have no choice but to marry, and "marry on whatever terms their masters have willed, or starve."[6] Secondly, the idea of a marriage contract is a falsehood because a husband and wife, unlike parties to true contracts, cannot agree to revise or alter its terms; they cannot, for example, (in 1825) agree to make the contract dissoluble. Nor, most fundamentally, can they agree to alter the po-

5. W. Thompson, *Appeal of One Half the Human Race, Women, Against the Pretensions of the Other Half, Man, to Retain them in Political, and Thence in Civil and Domestic, Slavery* (Source Book Press, New York, 1970), p. 55; pp. 66–7. (Originally published 1825).

6. Thompson, *Appeal*, p. 57.

sition of "wife" and "husband" constituted through the contract. However much a man may wish to do so he cannot give up the legal powers of a husband. Thompson is careful to point out that not all husbands exercise their power to its full extent; in effect he draws a distinction between the actions of individual husbands and the power embodied in the structure of the institution of marriage. Some husbands may, as he puts it, allow their wives equal pleasure to their own. However, the wife's enjoyment depends entirely on the benevolence of her husband and what he does, or does not, *permit* her to do. If a husband chooses to forgo all his legal powers, his wife still has "but the pleasures of the slave, however varied"[7] because her actions are always contingent upon the permission of the husband. Thompson claims that in some ways wives are worse off than the female slaves of the West Indies. For instance, a wife has to undergo "the gratuitous degradation" of having voluntarily to agree to her subjection when she vows obedience.[8] There is at least no pretense about the fact that female slaves are forced into slavery: there is, one might say, no talk of the slave contract.

The marriage contract is criticized less polemically, but no less forcefully, four decades later in *The Subjection of Women.* John Stuart Mill was one of the rare men who not only supported the feminist movement but attempted to put his sympathies into practice. Two months before he and Harriet Taylor were married in 1851, he wrote a statement rejecting the legal powers that he would acquire as a husband—though his rejection had no legal standing—undertaking "a solemn promise never in any case or under any circumstances to use them." He states that he and Taylor entirely disapprove of existing marriage law because it "confers upon one of the parties to the contract, legal power and control over the person, property and freedom of action of the other party, independent of her own wishes and will."[9] Mill follows Thompson quite closely in many of his arguments in the *Subjection.* He, too, argues that women have no alternative but to marry. "Wife" is the only position their upbringing and social and

---

7. Thompson, *Appeal,* p. 89.
8. Thompson, *Appeal,* p. 65.
9. Mill, *Essays on Sex Equality,* p. 45.

legal pressures realistically leave open to them, but to become a wife is tantamount to becoming a slave, and, in some ways, is worse. Mill, echoing Thompson, calls a wife the "actual body-servant of her husband: no less so, as far as legal obligation goes, than slaves commonly so called." He draws attention to the fact that a wife, unlike (in principle at least) a female slave, has no right "to refuse to her master the last familiarity. . . . [she can be] made the instrument of an animal function contrary to her inclinations."[10] Mill also distinguishes between the behavior of individual husbands and the structure of the institution of marriage. He argues that defenders of the marriage law rely on the example of husbands who refrain from using their legal powers, yet marriage is designed for every man, not merely a benevolent few, and it allows men who physically ill-treat their wives to do so with virtual impunity.

Mill does not explicitly argue that the marriage contract, given its structure and consequence, is not properly a contract. Rather, he calls for reform of marriage law to bring the marriage contract in line with other contracts. He notes that "the most frequent case of voluntary association, next to marriage, is partnership in business," but marriage compares very unfavorably with business. No one thinks that one partner in a business must be absolute ruler; nobody would enter a business partnership if that were the case. Theory and experience both confirm that the appropriate arrangement is for the conditions of partnership to be freely negotiated in the articles of agreement. Similarly, Mill argues, in marriage the "natural arrangement" is a division of powers between husband and wife, "each being absolute in the executive branch of their own department, and any change of system and principle requiring the consent of both." How is the division to be made? Mill suggests, on the one hand, that it will be freely agreed according to the capacities of the partners; they could "pre-appoint it by the marriage contract, as pecuniary arrangements are now often pre-appointed."[11] On the other hand, as feminist critics have recently pointed out, Mill is ultimately inconsistent in his argument. When discussing the tasks of a wife he falls back on the appeals to custom and

10. Mill, "Subjection," p. 158; p. 160.
11. Mill, "Subjection," pp. 168–9.

nature that he explicitly rejects earlier in the *Subjection*. Mill assumes that when women have equal opportunity in education, and marriage has been reformed so that husbands are no longer legally sanctioned slave masters, a woman, by virtue of becoming a wife, will still "choose" to remain in the home, dependent on her husband. He thus assumes that in this fundamental matter the *content* of a freely negotiated contract would reproduce patriarchal status. However, despite Mill's reluctance to take his attack on status to its logical conclusion, the general direction of his argument is that marriage must become a proper contract.

Many of the reforms of marriage law demanded by Thompson and Mill have now been enacted. The legal position of a wife in Anglo-American jurisdictions has been transformed from that of a legal non-person, the property of her husband, to near civil equality with her spouse. Nevertheless, recent feminist argument stresses that the marriage contract still diverges in significant respects from other contracts, illustrating a striking continuity in feminist criticism over one hundred and fifty years.[12] Liberal principles, and the safeguards developed for parties to contracts in other areas, still do not fully apply to the marriage contract. Feminists emphasize two areas in particular: first, the individual right of self-protection. Usually it is held that a valid contract cannot require that one party relinquish the right of self-

---

12. For the argument in the text see S.A. Ketchum, "Liberalism and Marriage Law," in *Feminism and Philosophy*, (ed.), M. Vetterling-Braggin, F.A. Elliston and J. English (Littlefield, Adams, New Jersey, 1977), and D.L. Barker, "The Regulation of Marriage: Repressive Benevolence," in *Power and the State*, (ed.), G. Littlejohn, B. Smart, J. Wakeford and N. Yuval-Davis (Croom Helm, London, 1978). For a discussion of the empirical evidence on the deleterious effects of marriage for women, see J. Bernard, *The Future of Marriage*, (Bantam Books, New York, 1974). Another contemporary feminist argument about the marriage contract is that it is really a labor contract through which husbands appropriate the unpaid work of their wives; see C. Delphy, "Continuities and Discontinuities in Marriage and Divorce," in *Sexual Divisions and Society*, (ed.), D.L. Barker and S. Allen, (Tavistock, London, 1976). I have discussed this argument in an unpublished companion essay "Wives, Slaves and Wage Slaves."

protection, but today, as in the nineteenth century in most legal jurisdictions, it is still deemed legally impossible for a husband to rape his
wife, and wives find it hard in practice to obtain proper legal protection against other forms of physical assault by their husbands.

The second peculiarity stressed by feminists is that the marriage
contract does not, like other contracts, exist as a written document that
is read and then signed by the contracting parties. Individuals usually
must be able to read and understand the terms of a contract before
committing themselves. In contrast, in marriage, a woman and man
are transformed into wife and husband through a ceremony and their
speech acts within it, not literally by signing a contract.[13] Moreover,
unlike other contracts, the marriage contract cannot be entered into
by any two (or more) sane adults but is restricted to two individuals,
who must be female and male, not related in prescribed ways, and so
forth. Nor can these two, as Thompson and Mill hoped, freely negotiate the terms of their contract; they do not even have a choice between several different contracts. Couples do have some scope for
making their own arrangements, but it is important to note that
Thompson's point about permission remains relevant; individual vari-
ations are made within "a relationship of *personal* dependency, the
couple work out together what the husband wants [the wife] to do . . .
within certain general parameters."[14] These "general parameters" are

---

13. In Australia, marriage celebrants now give potential spouses a leaflet,
"Marriage and You," issued by the Attorney General's Department, when
they give notice of marriage. The leaflet "tells you (1) something of what it
means to be married; (2) the duties of marriage; (3) about pre-marital education . . .; (4) about pre-marital counselling . . ." (I am grateful to Marian
Sawer for providing me with a copy of the leaflet). Strictly, a man and woman
become "husband" and "wife" after performing a speech act *and* having
sexual intercourse. The "marriage license" is not so much a contract as a li-
cence from the state and/or church to have sexual intercourse and procreate.
A priest recently refused to perform a marriage ceremony for a partially paralyzed man in Chicago because he was unable to have sexual intercourse; report in *Sydney Morning Herald,* 28 Jan, 1982. See the text below for comments on the bodily integrity of wives.

14. Barker, "The Regulation of Marriage," p. 242.

set by the structure of the institution of marriage. The essential feature of the marriage contract is that only a woman can have the rights and duties of a "wife" and only a man those of a "husband." In other words, the singular feature of the marriage contract is that it is a contract grounded in and maintaining status or ascription. Birth and the natural criterion of sex determines who can be a "wife" and "husband" and what each status entails. Today, as in 1825, the shamefulness of the marriage contract for feminists is that patriarchal status, the taken-for-granted, natural subjection of (women) wives to (men) husbands is confirmed through contract.

Barker has observed that the marriage contract "is not in fact a contract between the spouses, but rather they agree together to accept a certain (externally defined) status."[15] Although this statement points to the crucial fact that marriage is an institution of status or ascription, it fails to capture the full shame and contradiction of the marriage contract. If the marriage contract is not, as it appears to be, a contract between two individuals, the question immediately arises whether it is a contract at all. This may seem an odd question because marriage, according to the entry under "contract" in the *Oxford English Dictionary*, has been seen as a contractual relationship since at least the fourteenth century, and Blackstone wrote in his famous *Commentaries* in the eighteenth century, that "our law considers marriage in no other light than as a civil contract." But repeated references to the contractual character of marriage obscure more than they illuminate. For example, in the days of arranged marriages the contract was surely between the two (fathers of the) families, not the spouses. Now that marriage is what historians like to call "companionate" or "egalitarian," a voluntary matter between two individuals, rather than contracting together, the spouses are still agreeing or consenting to an externally prescribed status.

In one sense this has always been very well understood.[16] In the

---

15. Barker, "The Regulation of Marriage," p. 254.

16. In 1888 an American judge stated that "when the contracting parties have entered into the married state, they have not so much entered into a contract as into a new relation, the rights, duties and obligations of which rest not upon their agreement, but on the general law of the State, . . . it was of

1640s, "the 'contractual' element in marriage [was] simply the *consent* of each party to marry the other, . . . To contract a marriage was to consent to a status which in its essence was hierarchical and unalterable."[17] The failure to distinguish contract from consent has long been a major source of confusion in political theory, especially in discussions of the social contract. Logically, contract is the "beginning;" consent follows subsequently. (In the case of the social contract, consent is given—it is never refused in the contract story—by the "next generation" to the political arrangements constituted through the social contract of their fathers).[18] Ideologically, however, it is extremely useful to blur the distinction between the practices of contract and consent, and it is even more useful in the case of the marriage contract than the social contract. Almost everyone agrees that the social contract is merely an exercise in hypothetical reasoning or a political fiction, but it is never suggested that the marriage contract is a fiction. The marriage contract, it is confidently assumed, is entered into every day; it is an actual original contract for each pair of spouses. But this, as Thompson declared in 1825, is an "audacious falsehood." The conclusion to be drawn from the feminist critique of the marriage contract is precisely that it is a fiction. It is called a contract between a man and woman; the reality is that they consent to the patriarchally ascribed status of superior husband and subordinate wife. Or is this the reality? An examination of the status of "wife" reveals that the feminist

---

contract that the relation should be established, but being established, the power of the parties as to its extent or duration is at an end." Cited in K.G. McWalter, "Marriage as a Contract: Towards a Functional Definition of the Marital Status," *Columbia Journal of Law and Social Problems*, 9, 1973, p. 608.

17. Shanley, "Marriage Contract and Social Contract," p. 79. In the seventeenth century "contract seems to have been used more as a formal explanation of how people entered relationships than as a definition of the nature and content of these stations." G.J. Schochet, *Patriarchalism in Political Thought* (Blackwell, Oxford, 1975), p. 82.

18. The distinction between contract and consent, and its relevance for social contract theory and arguments about political obligation, is explored in detail in my *The Problem of Political Obligation* (Wiley, Chichester, 1979).

critique has not gone far enough. The contract is a fiction, but to re-place contract with consent, the consent of *both* spouses to their status, is to perpetuate a nice piece of political mystification. The presup-positions of the status of "wife" mean that it is not possible for a woman simultaneously to become a wife and to give consent.[19]

The social practices of contract and consent depend upon the pos-session of certain attributes and capacities by those engaged in them; both practices assume that participants are the "individuals" who ap-peared in liberal theory when the attack on status and the movement to contract began. They are individuals who are "naturally" free (and so can be governed only with their express agreement), who have a property in their person and capacities, and are political equals—and are men. Only during the past few years, as the organized feminist movement has begun to have an impact in academia, has attention be-gun to be focused on the accommodation of patriarchalism, or status, with liberalism, or contract, and the exclusion of women from the (ap-parently) universal categories of liberalism, including the "individ-ual." The exclusion has its roots in the mutual agreement between the social contract theorists and the patriarchalists that a wife's subjection to her husband had a natural foundation.[20] The depth of contempo-rary belief that this is the natural order of things is most starkly re-vealed in the legal right of a husband to rape his wife; central aspects of what has been called the "law of male sex right"[21] are enshrined in civil law and social practice. In other words, the status of "wife" is based on the denial that women are (or can be) "individuals." If a

19. The question of women and consent is discussed in more detail in my "Women and Consent," *Political Theory,* VII, 2, 1980, pp. 149–168.

20. On this agreement see T. Brennan and C. Pateman, " 'Mere Auxilia-ries to the Commonwealth': Women and the Origins of Liberalism," *Political Studies,* XXVII, 2, 1979, pp. 183–200.

21. A. Rich, "Compulsory Heterosexuality and Lesbian Existence," *Signs,* 5,4, 1980, p. 645. Social beliefs about the proper status of women are also well illustrated by the fact that in November 1979 in Dublin it was still possi-ble for a husband to sue successfully for damages under the law of "criminal conversation" if his wife committed adultery. *Report in New Statesman,* 2 May, 1980.

woman is to give consent to the status she is to acquire on marriage she must—naturally—have the rights and capacities of an "individual." However, it is logically impossible for a "wife" to possess these attributes because that would be simultaneously to claim that a woman is both naturally free and naturally in subjection. This contradiction is hidden under the fiction of the marriage contract and the mystification of consent; a gloss of free agreement is given to the shameful reality of the ceremonial confirmation of the ascribed, patriarchal subjection of wife to husband.

It might be objected that this extension of the feminist critique would have been all very well in 1825 or 1869 but it is misplaced in the 1980s when women are, at last, being recognized as "individuals." In New South Wales, for example, rape within marriage has become a criminal offense. In general, the reforms of the past decade are creating the social basis from which the marriage contract and women's consent can become a reality. The conception of "wife," it could be argued, is changing; the movement from status to contract is finally reaching into the institution of marriage. Marriage can, at last, become a properly contractual relationship, entered into on an equal footing by women and men who mutually and freely negotiate the terms of their contract. Ascribed patriarchal status will no longer determine rights and duties. Rather than dwelling on a status already receding into the past, the objection might continue, feminists should work to universalize contract as the general form of marriage. But is this the conclusion to be drawn from the feminist critique? Is contract the way to overcome the shame of status, of patriarchal subjection, within marriage? A consideration of Hegel's claim that an essentially contractual conception of marriage is itself shameful is necessary before it can be concluded that the apparently obvious solution is also a feminist solution.

The Marriage Contract that Transcends Contract

The conception of marriage as essentially contractual is part of the theoretical stock of liberalism. Locke, for example, states that "conjugal society" arises from a "voluntary Compact between Man and Woman," which establishes "such a Communion and Right in one

another's Bodies, as is necessary for its chief End, Procreation," and
"mutual Support and Assistance."[22] The keystone of the contractarian
view of marriage is the doctrine that individuals have "a right in one
another's bodies." The right follows from a conception of individuals
as owning the property they possess in their persons and bodies; one
individual can thus have rightful access to, or sexual use of, the body
of another only with the consent or agreement of, or through a contract with, the property owner. The marriage contract establishes legitimate access to the body of a spouse. Logically, the contract should
provide mutually equal access, but the patriarchal fiction of the contract hides the fact that the wife is excluded from the status of an "individual" who owns property in her person; hence, her body becomes
part of her husband's property, and the husband gains an unlimited
access to his wife's body and the wife no right at all.

In the *Philosophy of Right,* Hegel's critique of the contractual view
of marriage is directed against Kant. Kant explicitly presents marriage
as nothing more than a contract for mutual use of bodies, defining
marriage as the "union of two persons of different sex for the life-long
reciprocal possession of their sexual faculties."[23] Marriage, Kant argues, necessarily follows from the natural sexual attraction between a
woman and man. If they wish to have "reciprocal enjoyment" or "reciprocal use" of their bodies then they *must* marry each other. If they
do not marry, then, according to Kant, natural sexual feeling de-
humanizes the couple; sexual intercourse between unmarried individuals is "in principle . . . on the level of cannibalism."[24] Through marriage the couple can transcend mere sexual appetite and natural inclination and enter the realm of law and reason. Although each partner
acquires rightful use of the body of the other as if the spouse were no
more than a piece of property, Kant argues that through marriage, in
which the possession is mutual and reciprocal, each retains the status
of a person. Hegel attacks Kant precisely because, in his argument,

22. J. Locke, "Second Treatise of Government," in *Two Treatises of Government* (ed.), P. Laslett (Cambridge University Press, 1967), § 78.

23. Kant, *The Philosophy of Law* (trans.), W. Hastie, T & T Clark (Edin-
burgh, 1887), § 24, p. 110.

24. Kant, *Philosophy of Law,* § 31, p. 239.

marriage is "degraded to the level of contract for reciprocal use."[25] Such a view of marriage is shameful.

There are two related aspects to Hegel's critique of the contractarian conception of marriage. First, it is shameful because individuals are treated as if they were nothing more than owners of their physical bodies and sexual inclinations, so eliminating other aspects of human personality. Marriage becomes merely a way of avoiding sexual "cannibalism," or unauthorized use of bodies. Individuals then appear as if their whole beings were those of the makers of contracts and this is, for Hegel, to substitute a theoretical abstraction for the complex individuality of actual men and women. Hegel discusses contract under the heading of "Abstract Right" in the *Philosophy of Right* and argues that to see individuals purely as makers of contracts is to see them as "immediate self-subsistent persons,"[26] abstracted from their concrete social relationships. The perspective of contract presupposes that individuals are property owners, that each owner is recognized in this capacity by others and recognizes them in turn (that is, they each admit that others are of equal standing to themselves). The practice of contracting gives objective expression to this mutual recognition. When entering a contract two individuals "will" or share the common goal of exchanging their property to their mutual advantage. A contract enables them to make mutual use of each other—whether they are exchanging material goods or bodies.

Second, Hegel's criticism is that an essentially contractual view of marriage eliminates the qualitative distinction between the spheres of civil society and the family. Marriage and the family are shamefully treated as if they were an extension of civil society and so constituted by, and their relationships exhausted by, contract. Hegel agrees with Kant that it is our "objectively appointed end and so our ethical duty"[27] to marry, and thus establish a family. The contractarian conception leaves marriage open to the pure contingency, the whim and caprice, of sexual attraction, and gives rise to a superficial understand-

---

25. G.W. Hegel, *Philosophy of Right,* (trans.), T.M. Knox (Oxford University Press, 1952), Addition to § 161.

26. Hegel, *Philosophy of Right,* § 75.

27. Hegel, *Philosophy of Right,* § 162.

ing of the marriage contract as merely the public recognition and regulation of natural sexual inclination. Hegel argues that, on the contrary, a specific form of ethical life and association, that is, the family, is created through the marriage contract. The family is the most "immediate" dimension of ethical life, where individuals are members of an undifferentiated unity, or an association based on "love, trust, and common sharing of [the partners'] entire existence." The family has its origins in contract because marriage begins in contract; Hegel does not dispute this. However, Hegel claims that the marriage contract is a *unique* contract "to transcend the standpoint of contract."[28] One of the major theoretical aims of the *Philosophy of Right* is to show that transcendence of the standpoint of contract is necessary for the existence both of the family and the sphere of civil society. To fail to distinguish the contrasting principles of association of the two spheres is to fail to comprehend the social conditions for the existence of contract itself.

Hegel's critique of contractarian marriage is part of his much wider critique of liberal, abstract individualism, and thus goes deeper than an attack on its bleak view of individuals and their conjugal relations. The shame of contractual marriage arises from a lack of understanding of the social presuppositions of the sphere of contract. In order to enter a contract men must be "individuals" with a certain consciousness of themselves and their social relations (as property owners, equals, bearers of rights). But this, Hegel emphasizes, is only one dimension of social life and consciousness, and it is *because* it is a dimension, not the whole, that the contracts can be made. Any single contract presupposes the rule that the contracts must be kept, a rule involving trust and fidelity (which are constitutive of the bonds of family life). A single contract is possible, and individuals understand what it entails, only because it is part of the wider practice of contracting, which is constituted by the rule that contracts are binding. The social practice of contracting depends on an intersubjective understanding of what a contract is, and Hegel's discussion shows how the liberal conception of men as essentially makers of contracts both abstracts from, yet simultaneously takes for granted, this intersubjective understanding.

---

28. Hegel, *Philosophy of Right*, § 163.

"Contract" is socially meaningful precisely because consciousness is informed by conceptions and social relationships that are non-contractual. This wider consciousness cannot be developed within the sphere of contract itself.

Hegel's important argument about the social basis of contract can partly be expressed by distinguishing the "individual," who appears in abstract guise in liberal theory, from the individuality of actual women and men, a distinction crucial for an understanding of love as the principle of association of marriage and the family. To enter the marriage contract the spouses must be "individuals" conscious of the meaning of the social practice of contracting. However, the marriage contract "transcends the standpoint of contract," which implies that the wife and husband are not merely "individuals." Their individuality and consciousness must be developed in spheres other than that of contract if the marriage contract is to have its unique status. Without this wider and richer individuality they would remain trapped at the level of contract (indeed, strictly, "contract" would be meaningless to them), marriage could not transcend its contractual origin and they would have no comprehension of love. Hegel states that love is "the most tremendous contradiction."[29] It is contradictory because the lovers' first impulse is to want to obliterate their individuality in total unification with the loved one. In opposition to this desire, it is discovered that it is through the relationship with the beloved that individuality is strengthened and knowledge of the self as an autonomous person is gained. Love thus both unifies and differentiates; differentiation and individuality are created within the complex unity created by the bonds of love. The contradiction of love can be overcome by the mutual recognition that lovers give each other, through which each gains a deeper sense of their own autonomy. The social basis of love is strengthened by the dialectic of unification and differentiation, but none of this is possible within contractarian relations. In the latter, the spouses see each other from one perspective only, that of the mutual advantage of property owners, and no development of individuality can take place since the self is subsumed within the "individual" contract-maker. The bond between these selves can only be that of

_____

29. Hegel, *Philosophy of Right,* Addition to § 158.

mutual use—yet even this bond is illusory as it lacks the trust and faith necessary for its creation.

Before attempting to discuss the significance of Hegel's argument for feminist critiques of the marriage contract, it must be emphasized that his contract to transcend contract fails to overcome the shame of patriarchal subjection within marriage. The central place of mutual recognition in Hegel's account of love suggests that his argument is universal, that it includes both sexes. In fact, it applies only to men.[30] Hegel's claim that he has given "ethical significance" to the "difference in the physical characteristics of the two sexes"[31] is baseless; he sets women irrevocably outside of ethical life and so strips his theory of its necessary universal foundation. Struggle and "self-redemption" are necessarily required from men, outside of the family, in the development of their consciousness and individuality, but Hegel insists that women find their "substantive destiny" purely within the family. His patriarchalism blinds him to the fact that he has thus divided and separated the sexes not, as he claims, differentiated while uniting them. He thus destroys the grounding of his theory. From inside the family, the sphere of "immediacy," women can never develop the consciousness of "particularity" (that of the "individual") required if they are to enter a (marriage) contract. Nor can they develop the individuality necessary to give to and receive from a husband the recognition on which the dialectic of love and, hence, the bonds of the sphere of marriage and the family depend.

Hegel's unique marriage contract turns out to be just as much a patriarchal fiction as the mundane contracts of Locke or Kant. In one important respect Hegel also follows Kant rather than criticizing him. Kant makes much of the "relation of EQUALITY" in marriage between husband and wife, "as regards the mutual possession of their Persons, as well as of their Goods."[32] However, this is a mere appearance of

---

30. My comments in this paragraph have benefited from P.J. Mill's "Hegel and 'the Woman Question'; Recognition and Intersubjectivity," in *The Sexism of Social and Political Theory,* (ed.) L. Clark and L. Lange (Toronto University Press, 1979).

31. Hegel, *Philosophy of Right,* § 165.

32. I. Kant, *The Philosophy of Law,* § 26, p. 111.

equality. Kant rejects the suspicion that there is something contradictory about combining equality with the legal recognition of the husband as master. He states that this "cannot be regarded as contrary to the natural Equality of a human pair, if such legal Supremacy is based only on the natural superiority of the faculties of the Husband compared to the Wife . . . and if the Right to command is based merely upon this fact."[33]

Hegel's argument also attempts to combine equality with the right of command of the husband. His discussion suggests that, because marriage begins in a contract, the equal exchange that (it is claimed) takes place in other contracts also obtains between husband and wife and they thus recognize each other as equals. Indeed, the contractarian conception of marriage explicitly implies that such an exchange occurs; the spouses exchange the property in their persons and equality of access to each other's body is established. However, I have already noted that the status of "wife" means that such an exchange is impossible; rather the husband becomes owner of and master over the body of his wife. This reality is masked in Hegel's critique of the abstraction of the standpoint of contract because he sees no contradiction in a contract between a man who is an "individual" and a woman who is by nature unable to develop the capacities of an "individual." If there is any exchange embodied in the contract it consists of an exchange of obedience by the wife in return for protection by her husband[34]—except that no protection is afforded to a woman with the status of "wife." The contractarian conception of marriage and Hegel's unique marriage contract are both covered in shame.

Contract, Love and Friendship

The appeal of (properly) contractual marriage as a solution to the shame of the patriarchal subjection of wives is hardly unexpected when women have only so recently won major advances in the struggle for practical social recognition as "individuals." The solution also

---

33. Kant, *Philosophy of Law*, p. 112.

34. For the argument that this is the paradigmatic form of exchange in liberalism, see my *The Problem of Political Obligation*.

has popular, commercial backing in numerous advice books on marriage and sexual matters.[35] However, because women are finally being admitted as "individuals," the full implications of contractarianism, or the full implications of completing the movement from status to contract, are becoming apparent. The theoretical implications were spelt out in Hegel's philosophical and sociological critique of the standpoint of contract and abstractly individualist liberalism. To attempt to replace status by contract alone is to assume that the example of a single contract can be generalized so that social life as a whole is constituted through contract, or is a series of mutually advantageous exchanges between individuals. The argument of the *Philosophy of Right* is that this assumption is incoherent, and that the movement from status to contract cannot be taken to its logical conclusion. The standpoint of contract is unable to provide a coherent basis for social order. Without extra-contractual social relations and consciousness, which are explicitly rejected by the standpoint of contract, contract itself is impossible. Hegel's general critique of contract might seem far removed from feminist attacks on the marriage contract. Yet, when feminists point to the divergences between the marriage contract and other contracts this inevitably suggests (in the absence of argument to the contrary) that they are looking to a contractarian alternative. Feminism thus appears to lie firmly within the logic of the movement from status to contract. But if this is the case, feminists are relying on a theoretical perspective that, ultimately, can give no grounding for a feminist social order, and on a conception of social and sexual relationships with practical implications that run counter to central values and ideals of feminism.

Despite the enormous theoretical strength of the Hegelian critique of the abstract basis of contract doctrine, general theoretical argument has done little to impede the spread and consolidation of contractarianism. However, this is not surprising, since contractarianism is not a purely theoretical matter. "Contract" originated in a revolutionary

---

35. On the advice manuals see E. Ross, " 'The Love Crisis': Couples Advice Books of the Late 1970s," *Signs,* 6,1, 1980, pp. 109–122: also B. Ehrenreich and D. English, *For Her Own Good: 150 Years of the Experts' Advice to Women* (Anchor Press, New York, 1978).

challenge to traditional ties of status between males, and contractual conceptions helped constitute the institutions of the new, liberal society. But contractarianism is also the ideology of our society and, as the example of the marriage contract reveals, contract does not merely reflect but, more importantly, obscures the patriarchal structure of domination of liberalism. Feminists have noted, for example, that the advocates of "contract marriage" ignore the fact that it is open only to a few well-educated, professional women to negotiate as equals with men to draw up a mutually advantageous contract. The patriarchal structuring of the occupational hierarchy means that most women in the paid labor force earn considerably less than men, so they lack the power to bargain for a contract with an egalitarian content. Such practical objections and wider theoretical critiques nevertheless do little to detract from the success of contract as ideology; "questions about the theoretical coherence of contractarianism need not affect its ideological coherence, except insofar as they become questions in the minds of its adherents."[36] Examples of times and places when questions have been asked can be found in the history of the socialist and feminist movements, but this has not been sufficient to develop a general, popular questioning consciousness. The revival of the organized feminist movement offers the possibility that "questions in the mind" could become widespread precisely because feminism is the political movement concerned with the way in which the structure of our individuality and personal lives is an integral part of the structure of liberal-patriarchal institutions. The theoretical and practical problems of the standpoint of contract are thus raised in their most acute form.

One of Hegel's objections to the view that marriage is no more than a contract is that it leaves marriage at the mercy of the whims and capricious wills of the contractors. Similarly, Durkheim, who also argues that "a contract supposes something other than itself," emphasizes that the bond created by contract is both external and of short duration; it leads to "transient relations and passing associations."[37] A contract of mutual advantage and reciprocal use will last only so long as it

---

36. Gauthier, "The Social Contract as Ideology," p. 156.

37. E. Durkheim, *The Division of Labour in Society* (Free Press, New York, 1964), p. 381; p. 204.

appears advantageous to either party. A new contract with a different partner, will always appear as a possible and enticing alternative. The way in which popular advice books present divorce illustrates this very well; divorce is seen as something that can be "pre-considered in terms of personal upward mobility, with stress . . . on what lies ahead that may be incorporated into a new and better image."[38] A contract of mutual use could specify that the contractors will become parents— but how exactly do contractarians see the relation of child to parents? Hobbes was the only classic contract theorist willing to sweep away the last stronghold of status and take contract to its logical conclusion. He interpreted the dictum that we are "born free and equal" quite literally and argued that the relation of child to parent was conventional or contractual. A consistently contractual conception of marriage must hold that, immediately children reach the age (however young that may be judged to be) at which they are capable of making a contract with their parents, they should do so. Or, if the parents cannot offer a sufficiently advantageous contract, the child must be free to contract with other adults. This view may have its attractions when contrasted with the idea that parents have a property in their children, but it is extremely doubtful whether the transitory, external bonds of mutual use and advantage between adults, and between adults and children, could provide the necessary social foundation for children to develop a secure self-identity and individuality, even a self that is purely the self of a contractor.

The social conditions within which human beings can develop and flourish are formed by the non-contractual relationships that contractarianism attempts to eliminate. There is no place for love within the standpoint of contract, unless, that is, it is reduced to no more than

---

38. Cited in Ehrenreich and English, *For Her Own Good,* p. 276, (from H. Newberger and M. Lee, *Winners and Losers*). Another writer comments: "How better to alienate individuals from their identities than to treat them as business associates in a contract entered into exclusively on the basis of benefits received—entered into solely to enhance the private interests of the contracting parties . . . The real point of the modern marriage contract is to anticipate and provide for divorce . . . ." B. Barber, *Liberating Feminism* (The Seabury Press, New York, 1975), pp. 62–3.

sexual inclination and satisfaction. For Kant, marriage *is* the right to another's body or the reciprocal use of the property in a spouse's person. This chill reductionism is illustrated in a recent example of the way in which "radical contractarianism has come more and more to dominate our thoughts and actions."[39] An economic account of marriage claims that love is a "particular non-marketable household commodity"[40]—which can thus enter into the calculation of mutual advantage when entering the marriage contract. Love, in the sense of bodily use, is clearly marketable, or it could not form part of the contract, and one does not have to believe that sexual pleasure is somehow inherently immoral, or that it can never on occasions be proper to seek no more than sexual pleasure, to agree with Hegel that there is something shameful about this idea of marriage. The widespread marital and non-marital use of women's bodies has led feminists to claim that "the sexual revolution is not our revolution;"[41] it may thus seem puzzling that there is also a long history of feminist criticism of love.

Feminists have attacked love since at least 1792 when Mary Wollstonecraft stated that she would commit "high treason against sentiment and fine feelings" by writing disrespectfully of love.[42] Feminists have strongly criticized both the marriage contract which gives the husband unlimited access to the body of his wife, and romantic love, a particular form of love, or ideology of sentiment, that helps maintain the fiction of the marriage contract and obscure the reality of the patriarchal subjection of wives. In earlier feminist critiques of marriage and love, friendship is seen as the alternative, egalitarian basis for conjugal relations. Recent writers usually refer to love rather than friendship, although it has been suggested that if marriage is seen "non-instrumentally" then it is "a gesture of friendship."[43] The con-

39. Gauthier, "The Social Contract as Ideology," p. 159.

40. G.S. Becker, "A Theory of Marriage: Part II," *Journal of Political Economy*, 82, 2, Pt. II, 1974, p. 12.

41. I. Diamond, "Pornography and Repression: A Reconsideration," *Signs*, 5,4, 1980, p. 701.

42. M. Wollstonecraft, *A Vindication of the Rights of Women* (Norton, New York, 1975), p. 27.

43. L. O'Driscoll, "On the Nature and Value of Marriage," in M. Vetterling-Braggin (ed.), *Feminism and Philosophy*, p. 256.

temporary feminist non-romantic view of love is sketchily presented, but it has some striking similarities to the earlier idea of friendship between wife and husband. Shanley has recently argued that Mill's *Subjection of Women* is fundamentally concerned not with legal reform but "the hope of establishing friendship in marriage."[44] Mill's criticism of marriage displays the ambiguity characteristic of his social and political thought as a whole. If one strand of his argument suggests that marriage as a proper contract is the solution to the slavery of wives, he also offers hints of another conception of marriage. He looks to a relationship no longer based "in the instinct of individuals for self-protection, but in a cultivated sympathy between them," a relationship which would be a "school of sympathy in equality, of living together in love, without power on one side and obedience on the other."[45] At the end of the *Subjection*, when Mill turns to the "ideal of marriage," his discussion echoes Mary Wollstonecraft, for he writes of friendship, not love. A sympathetic association between the sexes will, he argues, lead to "a real enriching of the two natures." Mill notes that such enrichment can now occur between friends of the same sex, and in marriage, too, "a foundation of solid friendship" could provide the basis for "that best kind of equality, similarity of powers and capacities with reciprocal superiority in them."[46]

Shanley notes that Mill's ideal does not encompass "the possible enhancement which sexuality might add to marital friendship."[47] Both Wollstonecraft and contemporary feminists emphasize this enhancement, but without falling back on the contractarian view of marriage as an exchange of property and use of bodies. While rejecting the corrupt emotion of romantic love, born of domination and subjection, contemporary feminists see (real) love rather as Wollstonecraft saw friendship. They argue that love is possible only between equals, and refer to the mutual enrichment and enlargement of personality

---

44. M.L. Shanley, "Marital Slavery and Friendship: John Stuart Mill's *The Subjection of Women*," Political Theory, 9,2, 1981, p. 229.

45. Mill, "Subjection," p. 174, p. 175.

46. Mill, "Subjection," p. 234; p. 235.

47. Shanley, "Marital Slavery and Friendship," p. 243.

which love can bring, and the mutual esteem and respect on which it is based.[48] Thus the feminist alternative to the fiction of the marriage contract is a relationship resembling Hegel's non-contractual love. It is significant that we have no word for such a relationship. "Marriage" is too inextricably tied to the past of fiction and patriarchal subjection to be used for a sexually egalitarian partnership; I shall refer to the latter as personal association. Perhaps it does not matter in the end whether the bond constitutive of personal association is called love or friendship. (The earlier feminist theorists may have turned to "friendship" because philosophers have traditionally claimed that women naturally lacked the capacities that would enable them to be men's friends.) Hegel's dialectic of love, which has nothing romantic about it and which includes sexual passion, is, despite his patriarchalism, a crucial source for the development of a feminist theory and practice of personal association in which the bond of love and mutuality enables two individuals to "recognize" each other and enrich their union and individuality. However, a question remains about the creation of this bond. Perhaps, as Hegel argues, the marriage contract (its shameful past behind it) could find its rightful place as the public acknowledgment of the mutual trust, respect and love of the partners or friends; marriage would still be the contractual origin of a non-contractual association.

Beyond Status and Contract

Hegel claims that the marriage contract is a unique contract which transcends the practice of contracting. But why, it may be asked, introduce anything so paradoxical: why is it necessary for contract to enter into a non-contractual sphere of life? Hegel's reason for retaining the marriage contract is to ensure that individual freedom, in the sense of "particularity," or the "individual" aspect of individuality, finds a place in all spheres of the ethical life of the community. His attempt

---

48. See, for example, G. Greer, *The Female Eunuch* (MacGibbon and Kee, London, 1971), especially, pp. 139–245, and S. Firestone, *The Dialectic of Sex* (Bantam Books, New York, 1971), chs. 6 and 7; compare S. de Beauvoir, *The Second Sex* (Penguin Books, 1972), Part VI, 2.

founders with his separation of the sexes, but it is important to draw attention to the assumption underlying his argument: that a fundamental aspect of freedom can find expression only through contract. The assumption means that personal freedom becomes bound up with contract and hence with the abstract idea of the "individual." Valuable dimensions of personal freedom are then interpreted in one particular way, which appears as the only plausible interpretation. Bodily integrity, control of our bodies, is central to personal autonomy, to the ability to say "yes" and "no" and decide for ourselves how our personal lives will be ordered, and it appears that, if this dimension of freedom is to be given its proper weight, women and men must be seen as "individuals" and their relationships must take a contractual form. The alternative to a husband's patriarchal right to his wife's body thus appears to be the extension to women of ownership of the property in their persons. It seems that freedom necessarily entails ownership of the property in one's self and attributes, and that there are no alternative interpretations of personal autonomy; the shame of patriarchal subjection is replaced by the shame of contract and the ideology of contractarianism remains unquestioned.[49]

Attempts by critics of contract and abstract individualism to formulate a conception of the person as an essentially social being, with a developing and complex individuality, have invariably failed to break free of patriarchal assumptions, and are thus of limited assistance to feminist theorists. At best, conjugal relations and the physical reproduction of the next generation have been disregarded in discussions of freedom, autonomy and individuality. Against this theoretical background, and in the face of the many practical ways in which women have been and continue to be denied bodily integrity, the claim that women, too, own the property in their persons and thus have right of control over their bodies is of obvious importance. The crucial question, though, is whether feminism can go beyond this view and develop a non-contractarian conception of autonomy and bodily integ-

---

49. One consequence of the view that women have a property in their persons and bodies is that their right to sell their bodies in the market is established. I have criticized a contractarian defence of prostitution in "Defending Prostitution: Charges Against Ericcson," *Ethics*, 93, 3, 1983.

rity. This difficult task remains to be completed, but while feminist theorists can draw upon the insights of the great critics of the standpoint of contract, a feminist conception of individuality will differ from previous formulations because it will be both egalitarian and grounded in the fact that humankind has two bodies—and only women's bodies become pregnant. In a personal association, ascription or status will no longer determine the activities of the partners, so that childrearing will cease to be the responsibility of women alone, but it does not follow that the meaning of bodily integrity and autonomy will be exactly the same for women as for men. Bodily integrity for women can never be separated from the question of physical reproduction, so that, as Petchesky has pointed out,[50] a tension will always exist between autonomy and mutuality.

However, it might still be argued that, even though the abstractions of the standpoint of contract have been replaced by a social conception of individuality and mutuality, personal association can still, as Hegel claims, begin in a contract. I earlier remarked upon the failure by political theorists to distinguish consent from contract, and Hegel's argument about personal freedom and contract foreshadows a much wider contemporary tendency to identify with contract the many different ways in which women and men can freely make agreements and so bind themselves into the future. It is usually assumed that contracting exemplifies such activities, which provides a clear indication of how far the movement from status to contract and the consolidation of the ideology of contractarianism have advanced. The identification of, for example, agreeing, consenting, assenting, and promising with contract systematically shuts off exploration of non-contractual conceptions of social relationships and their political significance, and identifies the social creativity of free agreement with contract. Once contract is distinguished from other ways of agreeing and making commitments, it becomes clear that there is no necessity for personal association to have its origins in a contract. On the contrary, personal association begins in a promise. A contract of mutual use or an exchange of property in bodies excludes the trust and love that are fun-

---

50. R.P. Petchesky, "Reproductive Freedom: Beyond 'A Woman's Right to Choose,' " *Signs*, 5,4 1980, pp. 661–685.

damental to personal association, whereas a promise presupposes fidelity. I have discussed elsewhere the way in which promising rather than contract exemplifies the social creativity made possible through the practice of free agreement,[51] and it is by making a promise that two autonomous, loving partners can create a new relationship between themselves that mutually binds them into the future. Their voluntary, reciprocal commitment (or obligation) is the concrete, public expression of their love. By creating a personal association they constitute the bonds of mutuality within which they can maintain and enhance their autonomy and individuality through the dialectic of love.

The creation of a personal association does not, however, take place in social abstraction, nor do women and men exist only as members of personal associations. Personal association is one dimension of social life and can be fully understood only in the context of its place in a wider communal whole (just as Hegel's conception of the family is integral to the social whole of family–civil society–state). Differentiation, individuality and mutuality within personal association reflects the wider social context of a differentiated community. The liberal conception of the property-owning "individual" attempts to separate individuality from sociality and mutuality. The assumption underlying this attempt is that all social ties are of the same kind; all dimensions of social life are constituted by contract. In this respect, contract is not so much a movement from status as its negation or mirror image. The undifferentiated social bonds of a hierarchy of ascription are replaced by the undifferentiated, universal bond of contract. One of Hegel's profoundest insights and greatest theoretical legacies is the conception of a differentiated social order in which the various spheres of social life each rest on their own principle of association, or, to use Rawls' terminology, each have their own virtue. Love and

---

51. Promising and its creative potential is discussed in detail in my *The Problem of Political Obligation,* especially chs. 1 and 2. There are circumstances in which promises, though binding, may justifiably be broken. Similarly, there will be circumstances in which personal associations will be dissolved. It does not seem fruitful to advocate greater legal, or state, impediments to ensure a longer-lasting (reformed) marriage as Barber suggests. (*Liberating Feminism,* pp. 143–4).

promising are the virtue of personal association, but this is only one dimension of social life and other forms of association are grounded in their own principles or morality. Moreover, the mutuality of personal association presupposes that the social conditions exist, or are being created, that enable autonomous partners to enter into this commitment. Women and men cannot maintain their autonomy and individuality within personal associations if they are not also full and equal members of economic associations and equal citizens in political life. The transformation of marriage into feminist personal association thus presupposes, and is presupposed by, a similarly radical transformation of the patriarchal social structure of our economic and political life. The implications of this wider social transformation lie outside the scope of this essay, but a brief comment must be made about the conception of a differentiated social order.

I have argued that contract is unnecessary in personal life to give expression to autonomy and individuality. There is no need to introduce the mysteries of contracts that transcend contract. However, Hegel argues that contract is the virtue or principle of association of a specific sphere of social life; contract finds its proper place in civil society or economic life. This raises the complex (and virtually uncharted) question of what "differentiation" involves. Must the principles of association that constitute a differentiated social order be contrasting or even opposing principles, in the manner in which love and promising stand in opposition to contract, or is it possible to have a social whole of non-contractual, yet differentiated, principles? In *The Problem of Political Obligation,* I argued that (non-contractual) political obligation is the virtue of participatory democratic political life, and the political counterpart of promising. The non-contractual counterparts of love and mutuality are community and solidarity,[52] but the problem remains whether, if contract is rejected in personal and political life, a

---

52. Solidarity is not precisely right, since it is extremely doubtful if "solidarity," "comradeship" and similar terms include women. Women are usually auxiliaries to the male comrades and spectators of their solidarity. That it is so hard to find political concepts that encompass both sexes reflects the masculine character of the political itself, analyzed by Nancy Hartsock in this volume.

vital aspect of personal and collective freedom is also being rejected. Liberalism, of course, insists that contract is necessary and liberals find support today from the advocates of market socialism. The difficulty here is that little discussion is available of potential alternatives to the authoritarian structure of the command economy on the one hand, and contract, whether embodied in the capitalist or socialist market, on the other. This closure of possibilities resembles the alternatives of patriarchal subjection or contract found in discussions of the marriage contract. There is a parallel failure to recognize the significance of the critique of the standpoint of contract for the democratic restructuring of economic life, or that status, instead of being negated, might be transcended. If the argument has any force that autonomy in personal and political life can be upheld and furthered—indeed, can only be universalized—within a non-contractual association, then it does not seem implausible to suggest that a similar non-contractual alternative may be available in economic life. The major conclusion to be drawn from a critique of the shame of the marriage contract is that the theory and practice of a feminist social order lies beyond both status and contract.

5
WOMEN AND AUTHORITARIAN REGIMES

Fanny Tabak
Pontificia Universidade Catolica
Rio de Janeiro, Brazil

Women and Authoritarian Regimes
Fanny Tabak

Authoritarian Regimes

In Latin America during the last two decades, especially in the 70s, a recrudescence of authoritarianism and takeovers by military governments was observed even in some countries where a tradition of democratic practice had existed for many years. Such was the case of Chile and Uruguay. Even in those countries, military coups took place and constitutional governments were overthrown. Terrorism became a general rule, as did strict censorship and the torture and murder of people who opposed the new regimes.

The existence of hundreds of thousands of political exiles spread all over the world and the "disappearance" of party activists or people who were merely suspected of opposing those extremely authoritarian regimes became a common fact in the daily life of those countries. For years and years the migration from one country to another of highly qualified professionals resulted in a considerable waste of know-how which had been obtained, thanks to considerable effort and sacrifice, in countries which were still developing.

Authoritarianism is connected, in such countries, with military governments, which took over after coups and are an expression of the armed forces, i.e., those sectors of society which have arms at their disposal, control information and are acquainted with modern technology. Actually, military authoritarianism and repressive govern-

101

ments are no monopoly of Latin America, since many other countries might be pointed out, e.g. Greece and Turkey.

We should not forget that those governments are always composed of men—there is no example of a military junta headed by women. This fact is easy to understand, as we know that almost always and everywhere men make up the armed forces, possess arms, and command battalions, armies and divisions with the legal right to use violence.

Female participation in armed struggles has overwhelmingly been *against* authoritarianism and fascism. Women have not tried to overthrow constitutional governments and replace them by authoritarian regimes. It should be mentioned that women's role in the struggles for national liberation during World War II and presently among the guerrillas in Central America serves as a clear demonstration of women's capacity for combat.

One of the important questions that have been studied by political scientists is related to the conditions that give rise to authoritarian regimes. Actually, what do we mean by authoritarian regimes?

There seems to be no doubt about the general features of these regimes: they "reject even the basic principles of the bourgeois political democracy," says Chirkin.[1] At a minimum they decree the end of political democracy, which means they prohibit the legal existence of workers' parties or even any party, they suspend the constitution, they govern by decree, and they replace general elections with straight appointment of public officers.

The government uses predominantly open coercion instead of indirect (disguised) coercion. A number of pseudomilitary organizations are created to realize a violent repression of those who oppose the regime. Social demagogy and sophisticated techniques of ideological indoctrination are now widely used, although the main instrument is open and merciless violence.

Authoritarian regimes despise public opinion and their strength depends entirely upon massive repression and active intervention in all

---

1. Veniamin Chirkin, "Authoritarian Regimes in Developing Countries: Social Indicators of Strength and Weakness," paper presented IPSA World Congress, Rio, 1982.

spheres of public life. The official party—whenever it exists—is but an addendum of the governmental apparatus. It is a new political system in which governmental decrees substitute for the constitution and fundamental rights are abolished or suspended.

Such regimes can count upon the support of large sectors of the population because they use slogans with great popular appeal—the struggle against terror (or subversion), against anarchy and against economic chaos. Such aims serve as an excuse for the coup. Once in power these regimes speak in the name of nationalism, which may sometimes become extremely exacerbated.

The standards adopted by authoritarian regimes are determined almost always by the social forces that give them support. It seems evident, though, that these regimes' strength is more apparent than real, since they do not have deep social roots. Their strength is tied to the coercion they use against the people to keep them obedient.

These regimes' strength may be measured by their capability—usually existing for only a short time—of satisfying some of the population's basic needs while they turn toward their main goal—staying in power for the longest possible time.

Political evidence has shown that these regimes are able to keep power (to a great extent) due to the passivity of the fundamental classes in society. This passivity takes over either because the latter were unable to organize immediately after the coup and the replacement of a constitutional government by an authoritarian regime, or because the local bourgeoisie and the working class are still weak and lack the conditions to command resistance efficiently.

In the specific case of Latin America, it is not correct to say that authoritarianism has flourished in those countries where social and economic development are lowest. Such countries as Argentina and Chile were among those which had experienced impressive growth, a high level of trade unionism, a well-defined party structure, and political leadership with strong popular support. Nevertheless, military coups took place in those countries and strongly authoritarian regimes were established.

The same was true for Brazil, which is included among the more developed countries in the area and where military governments have succeeded each other since April 1964. It was only in December 1979 that the so-called period of "political opening" began, with an amnesty that has benefited thousands of political prisoners, exiles and prosecuted, as well as a new offering of the possibility of organizing new political parties (except the Communist Party which is still underground).

In fact, ideological and political issues are often the chief motivation (or justification) for the coups headed by military men who come from different sectors of the armed forces. The ghost of communism, subversion, terrorism, or guerrillas, the stress on safeguarding national security against "strange" or alien ideologies, the pretext of fighting corruption—all these are reasons offered by the leaders of coups, for overthrowing constitutional governments legally elected by the people.

Nonetheless, the recent political history of Latin American countries has demonstrated that strongly authoritarian and repressive governments are more corrupt than those they have replaced. Actually, it is easy to understand why, as they do not have to justify their actions and can stay in office without recall. The cases of Brazil and Argentina are illustrative. Argentina, one of the few countries in Latin America where the people had a high standard of living, was exactly the country where the military has seriously destroyed the national economy, creating an enormous foreign debt and a complete destruction of national industry.

In Brazil there have been an ever-increasing inflation (now over 100%), political and financial scandals, the devastation of public funds, and absurd privileges and favors granted people in government (which became known only after the strict censorship of the press was eased in December 1979).

It is easy to understand that relations between the state and civilian society in countries with authoritarian regimes were seriously affected. Such regimes resulted in a complete disarticulation of the society, which was prevented from organizing social strata and groups so that they could express their opinions. In many cases, the national congress was closed (as in Chile and Argentina) and political parties were prohibited. Of course, these actions resulted in a large step backwards, especially in countries with some sort of democratic tradition. In Chile and also in Uruguay—which actually were considered to be exceptions in the group of Latin American countries—democratic practice was much more representative before the coups of the 70s.

Some authors have tried to establish a relation between certain socioeconomic features of the countries where coups have taken place, e.g. high rates of rural–urban migration and the consequent concentration of large populations in metropolitan areas, which made it difficult to meet basic needs for public services. Resulting popular dissatisfaction and social agitation, or, as the authors of the coups used to say "social chaos," caused leaders to urge the establishment of a new social "order," one which was necessarily authoritarian.

To understand correctly the many forms of political domination in different Latin American countries considered "bureaucratic–authoritarian states," it is necessary to define the political role played by the military in the state apparatus. A great number of Latin American political scientists have tried to analyze such bureaucratic–authoritarian states, and the bibliography on this subject is extensive. One of the most creative authors is Guillermo O'Donnell.[2] Among many other questions he examines some of the distinctions between the coups of the 60s (Brazil and Argentina) and those of the 70s (Argentina, Chile and Uruguay). He attempts to understand the visible and implicit motivations of such events, the role of political parties and guerrilla organizations, and the degree to which political activity among the popular sectors was regarded by the military as "a serious danger for the preservation of the existing social order." Simultaneously he analyzes the implications of the economic crisis existing in each of those countries at the moment of the coup.

According to O'Donnell, "during the 60s the military had predominantly preventive and restorative intentions in heading the coups, while in the 70s their orientation was much more radical," i.e. they wanted to stop a process that seemed to be one step from a total col-

2. Guillermo O'Donnell, *Modernización y autoritarismo* (Ed. Paidós, Buenos Aires, 1972); "Armies and Politics in Latin America," Abraham Lowenthal, ed. (New York: Holmes and Meier, 1976); "Estado y alianzas en la Argentina, 1956–1976," in *Desarrollo Economico,* 16 no. 64, enero-marzo, 1977; "Tensiones en el Estado burocratico–autoritário y la cuestión de la democracia," *Estudios CEDES* (Buenos Aires, 1978).

lapse of the society, the economy, and the state, and that "required much more than just a restoration of a preexistent social order."[3]

Since the country faced a situation of crisis, the leaders of the coup were assured support from large social sectors, especially the local bourgeoisie, whose interests were defended. Thus the middle strata, who felt threatened by the popular sector's political agitation, the extremely high inflation rates, and the extent of public services, tended to support the authoritarian regimes which resulted from these coups.

In the specific case of Brazil (1964) one of the determinant factors for the coup was the alleged rupture of the military hierarchy inside the army. This could serve as an explanation (according to some authors) for the violent repression after the coup. In Uruguay and Argentina, the military were the target of guerrilla action and the violence of the coup was explained as retaliation.

O'Donnell ascribes great importance to the role of the technocrats as a right wing force which offered the military a political ideology under the cover of a political economy. At the same time, technocrats are the representatives of transnational financial capital in their own country.

One of the basic elements of that political ideology is the doctrine of national security, that expresses an "organic idea" of society, according to which that society is a body, each part of which fulfills clearly defined and hierarchically oriented functions. Such an ideology gives political identity to the armed forces, which become a main defender of national interests or even the expression and synthesis of such interests. To defend those interests means to fight subversion.

Manuel Garreton examined the ideological trajectory of that new authoritarian state in Latin America, which was connected with a virtual elimination of many important sectors of society, a strict censorship, the impossibility of free organization and many other extremely repressive decisions.[4]

---

3. Guillermo O'Donnell, "Las fuerzas armadas y el Estado autoritário del Cono Sur de América Latina," XXV Reunião Anual do Grupo "Armed Forces and Society" (Chicago, 1980).

4. Manuel Garreton, "De la seguridad nacional a la nueva institucionali-

As to women: authoritarian regimes have always regarded women as reproducers of traditional and conservative values, and have emphasized their role in the family as socializers of younger generations. They know quite well that it is in the family that children begin to receive political socialization (whatever political system is in force and no matter how crucial may have been the changes the family as a social institution has experienced). In spite of generational conflict and a new sort of relationship among family members, the influence of family structure on the political behavior of individuals has proven quite relevant.

Authoritarian regimes have always insisted on women's responsibility for not only the present but also the future behavior of their offspring. They insist on "order" and stability over disorder and political instability. They expect mothers to inculcate in their children such basic values as obedience and respect.

On the other hand, the political socialization of women in countries where authoritarian regimes have been the rule for decades (as is the case in Latin America) is greatly affected by illegal and antidemocratic policies. One of the most prejudicial of these policies is the lack of access to political information.

It is frequently asserted that women constitute a sound base of support for authoritarian regimes all over the world. Some authors refer to massive demonstrations where women express their approval of military coups. Indeed, some Latin American countries have given examples of such demonstrations in the last few decades. Still, the so-called female support for authoritarian regimes is sometimes too easily accepted as truth; this is only because some crucial aspects of political participation are neglected. First, it should be mentioned that men also support such regimes and are actually responsible for their establishment and continued existence. It is always men who seize power as a result of coups, and members of military governments are always men, not women. As for the conservative orientation in polls, that is not monopolized by women—men (millions of them) oppose social and political change, revolution and socialism.

---

dad. Notas sobre la trayectoria ideologica del nuevo Estado autoritário," in *Revista Mexicana de Sociologia,* no. 2, 1978.

The point is that women's role in the struggle for social and political change has been either minimized or ignored by historians and political scientists. Feminists consider it one of their main tasks to bring out the hidden history of women; i.e. the study of women as actors (in politics) and not just as passive objects obedient to men's commands. Nevertheless, the fact remains that many women do support, although they do not create or control, reactionary regimes.

Why Do Some Women Support Authoritarian Regimes?

Large sectors of the female population support authoritarian regimes in spite of the damage they cause to women. They do so for a variety of reasons. Some of these reasons were mentioned by participants in a discussion held in Chile in 1981 after a plebiscite which extended President Pinochet's term for another five years (75 percent of women said "yes").

A first point to be made is the low proportion of women who are economically active (seldom over 30 percent) in most countries where authoritarian regimes are in force. This means that most women are engaged only in housework. At the same time, there is a strong social devaluation of such work. Feminist movements began to emphasize the social significance of this fact during the 70s, but the fact that millions of women are still kept apart from the labor market means that they are not active in political and public life. Thus it is no surprise that women respond to and fall under the influence of governments which address them in the name of (the highly valued) family and motherhood.

According to the ideology of authoritarian regimes women's main social responsibility is to be "good" mothers, i.e. not only to fulfill their basic biological function as reproducers of human beings, but to reproduce as well ideological and social values. Pinochet's speech addressed to women insists that their task is to raise obedient citizens. Included is the idea that women should be prepared to support any sacrifice in order to help their government in difficult situations. Actually this may mean simply that they should avoid any sort of criticism or disruption of the status quo. In this connection, the armed forces are said to play a crucial role as guardians of the family's security and to be more reliable in doing so than politicians.

The so-called cultural conditioning of women which aims to prepare them to play their role of good wives and mothers contributes to a great extent to the conservative (resistant-to-change) views of some women. The stereotyped definition of sexual roles in society and the still prevailing, nonscientific assertions about women's intellectual inferiority to men most certainly contributes to reinforcement of the traditional image.

A great number of women in underdeveloped countries where authoritarian regimes exist are engaged in domestic work as servants in middle-class homes in big cities. They usually come from the countryside and constitute the larger proportion of wage-earning female workers in such countries. The impact of the "big town," the contrast between the values they bring from their original homes and the new morals of the home in which they work, and of the "home" in which they live, the continuous process of disaggregation of poor countryside families—all affect the migrant women to a considerable extent. No wonder prostitution grows among young female migrants.

In addition, middle-class urban values are frequently appropriated by rural-origin women, who see them as a means of social mobility and an improvement in their condition. That factor, then, might explain the conservative political attitudes of migrant women, who adopt the views of their employers.

If we consider that one of the main features of rural life is dispersion (or segregation), it is easier to understand how difficult it is for a migrant woman, who has lived isolated from the modern means of mass communication, to make political options. Peasant women are often not recognized as workers, nor do they receive any salary for their participation in agriculture in most underdeveloped countries. They have been accustomed all their lives to having someone (a man) make decisions for them. So, when they get to the "big town" it takes them a long time to learn to develop and assess options for themselves.

Another very important point must be made. While right wing parties have always had a clear policy towards women and have addressed them explicitly in language they understand, left wing parties in most countries (and that is the case for Latin America) have not troubled to deal with women's specific problems, nor have they tried to define what their policy would be.

Besides, progressive political parties, even those that have developed a consistent struggle against authoritarianism, have maintained a highly hierarchical structure. Women very seldom have had a chance to be in National (or Central) Committees where definition is given to party programs and electoral platforms. Moreover, the list of candidates for elections have been almost exclusively made by and composed of men.

As a matter of fact, political parties have often used women to "open" political space only to ignore women's needs once that was accomplished. When left wing labor parties speak of the labor force, they do not include women engaged in housework or domestic labor. Thus, these women hardly could agree that social change has anything to do with or for them.

There is another point. Many women who do join the "outside world," or labor market, and who perform professional activities (sometimes requiring very high qualifications) have not been liberated from domestic responsibilities. Their role as wife and mother is still considered their primary obligation. Thus, many of them are faced with an extremely difficult situation: they have to be simultaneously "good" mothers and wives and "very good" professionals (since they frequently have to prove they are better than men).

Such a situation can create a so-called guilt feeling, i.e. women professionals feel guilty towards their husbands and children for not dedicating to them all the working hours of the day. In other words, they "cause harm" to domestic life. Many women give up their professional activities when they get married or have small children as a result of all the social pressure. Some of them return to the labor market after their children are grown, but the long period of forced professional inactivity affects their performance and causes serious damage to their careers.

Another point should be mentioned. In many societies and presently in most underdeveloped countries, marriage is still considered the basic goal to be achieved by a young woman. So, the high social prestige awarded to a married woman (who was able to find a man to protect and support her) suggests that marriage is the more "secure" of the situations women could face. From a political point of view, that could serve to explain why so many surveys on electoral attitudes have shown that women tend to follow their husbands' preferences in voting.

There is still another point to consider if we want to understand support given by women to military regimes, especially if we are dealing with Latin American societies. Those are societies where a strongly authoritarian family structure is still the rule almost everywhere. Even in such countries where economic growth and modernization have already reached relatively high levels, countries where the urban population is larger than the rural, countries where industrialization has advanced to a considerable extent, the fact remains that cultural features prevalent over five decades are still quite evident. One of these features is the father as the holder of family authority. Very often it is unquestioned authority.

After marriage the authority of the father is replaced by that of the husband, even if there is no marriage celebrated according to the country's laws. The proportion of women capable of freeing themselves from such submission in the name of liberty and the right of autonomous decision-making is rather small. In spite of the growing number of women who graduate in all sorts of colleges, and no matter how much easier it becomes to work professionaly in occupations until recently considered "male" occupations, it is well known that any radical change in cultural traditions and habits occurs very slowly.

That is why millions of women are used to obeying orders given by a man—father, husband or political leader—and therefore acquiesce to a new government, no matter how authoritarian it may be. An authoritarian and repressive government able to maintain social "order" is even regarded by many women as an ideal government. One of the reasons always mentioned to explain the support Salazar had in Portugal for forty years was that he ruled over a "very clean" country, which certainly is related to many women's obsession with having their houses "proper and clean and shining."

But there are of course other explanations for the support afforded by large sectors of the female population to strongly repressive governments. Historical evidence has shown that such governments have been very successful in bringing women to their counterrevolutionary positions. Women who belong to the upper and upper-middle classes, who normally behave according to their husband's status, usually neither work professionally nor are engaged in housework (as they have servants for that). Thus they have been a stable basis of support for right wing movements. The impact of the "march of empty pans," conducted by women's organizations in Chile and Brazil was enormous, and those demonstrations contributed to the overthrow of both presidents Allende and Goulart.

As Gabriela Videla de Plankey pointed out, in Chile "the political forces who opposed Allende created the Female Power organization of housewives, professional women, public officers and commercial employees. Its political orientation was radical right wing and its leaders were relatives of politicians and military leaders who shared the same ideology."[5]

The first public demonstration of that Female Power was the "march of empty pans," at the beginning of December 1971 and was the sign for a violent campaign conducted by reactionary sectors against the contitutional government of the Popular Unity, headed by Allende. This was done in spite of the fact that Allende's government, one year before the march, had obtained 36.4 percent of the votes and the congress had confirmed him as president. Only six months before the coup, Allende had 44 percent of the polls, even though an economic and political crisis troubled the country.

The Forms of Women's Resistance To Authoritarian Regimes

Perhaps the most important forms of women's resistance to the cruelty of authoritarian regimes may be merely the ability to resist those regimes' continuous attempts to demoralize women, as mothers, wives, sisters and daughters. In their daily lives, in the privacy of their homes, in trying to preserve family unity and morale, in spite of all repression, torture, and murder (usual methods in the hands of authori-

---

5. Gabriela Videla de Plankey, "Las Mujeres pobladoras de Chile y el proceso revolucionario," in *Perspectivas Femininas en América Latina*, ed. Sepsetentas-Maria del Carmen Elu de Leñero (org.), 1976.

tarian regimes and military governments), women have been resisting for years.

Especially in Latin American countries known for their "machismo," women have had to face very often, sometimes for long periods, situations in which the man (husband, son or brother) who was "head of family" lost his job, "disappeared," was put in jail, or prosecuted or even murdered. In such cases, women had to resist and make sure that life could go on by looking after the children, by feeding them, making them go to school, socializing them—in a word, by preventing the moral disaggregation of the family unit.

Besides acting inside the strictly "private world," women were also the ones—in the absence of the "male" actor—to keep alive national values, national culture, historic traditions, respect for the country, in spite of all the evidence of corruption, moral disruption, cynicism, and opression. To maintain national dignity, traditions and values became in such situations a very important task, which women proved to be prepared to perform splendidly.

As a result, thousands of women in Latin American countries and elsewhere came to understand the close relation between their "private" lives and families and the whole political system. In many cases they had to take the place of husbands, fathers and brothers. That is how many of them became political activists, joined guerrillas or illegal parties, or liberation fronts. Political consciousness rose rapidly among many women who had never cared about politics and had once agreed—as they had been hearing all their lives—that "women understand nothing about politcs."

And in doing so, many women finally had the opportunity to demonstrate that they were as good in politics as their husbands, sons or brothers, killed, imprisoned or "disappeared." They finally had the chance to show that they were capable of more than just cooking, cleaning or looking after small children, that they could also hold guns, organize political demonstrations, fight to the death with guerrillas, make speeches to large rallies, and travel over the world to campaign for support against authoritarian regimes.

So, many wives who had been in a very secondary role while their husbands held office (one of the most striking examples is the wife of Chile's President Allende) suddenly came to the front of the stage and

113

revealed great strength and courage when their husbands were removed.

As always happens, dialectically, authoritarianism and repression served to develop many women's intelligence, creativity and political capacity. In the worst conditions of repression, when progressive political parties were banned and resistance had to go on, women discovered many different ways to face the situation.

But there is another relevant fact that should be mentioned. Women have resisted authoritarianism not only from inside, staying home, but also outside, i.e. abroad. Thousands of women have had to leave their countries to escape repression or murder. They are living sometimes thousands of miles away from their homes and relatives, forced to withstand extremely unfavorable conditions, as far as climate, language, standard of living, and job opportunities are concerned. Even under difficult conditions of political exile, culture and tradition expect women to take the same responsibility—even though the problems they have to face and solve were not created by them. Thousands of women who have never taken part in any political action have been forced to leave their countries and to accompany their husbands, fathers or sons. Living in a foreign country aggravates any feeling of guilt, frustration and anxiety that a woman might have and magnifies family problems, which she frequently must handle alone.

Women in exile have been playing a very important role by organizing protest groups and calling the attention of progressive forces and democratic governments to the critical situation created in many countries by authoritarian regimes and to the need to put an end to their repressive measures. Women have been organizing meetings, writing, speaking, taking advantage of whatever opportunity may arise for them to address large audiences in international conferences, world congresses, workshops. Women have created original and new forms of organizations to unite their forces and their skills and to give moral support to one another during the long periods of political exile. Most of them use the opportunity to improve their professional qualifications or to acquire new skills, as they understand they will be able to serve their country better when they are able to return.

It is particularly difficult to resist repression when you are a political prisoner; nonetheless, thousands of women sentenced or put in jail without trial have succeeded in resisting. "Women imprisoned by Latin American dictatorships in the last decades," says Luis Vitale, "had an exemplary behavior during the fight and an irreconcilable attitude in facing the torturers."[6] The torture techniques used in legal prisons as well as the illegal ones (linked with the many pseudomilitary organizations created by those governments) were always much more frightening for women than for men. Unthinkable forms of sexual violence were used against the female prisoners in an attempt to break their morale and force them to "confess" their political activity and to accuse other militants and activists.

Luis Vitale describes terrible forms of torture practiced against women while he was a "war prisoner," for a year and a half, in nine different torture houses and concentration camps created by Pinochet in Chile. He states that when "tortured, humiliated and violated massively, [women] have proved to be stronger and more resistant to pain than men." In 1973, soon after the coup that overthrew President Allende, more than one thousand women imprisoned inside the National Stadium were capable of keeping a high level of morale, of breaking through the isolation and finding means to establish contact with the men to offer them some form of consolation.

"A sociology of the daily life of political prisoners—which has not been written yet—would reveal the thousand and one forms of resistance invented by Latin American women in the dictatorships' prisons," says Vitale. Indeed, terrorist methods of physical torture and all sorts of humiliation used by reactionaries have been unable to stop the fight conducted by democratic women against those regimes.

Other women have helped to fight military dictatorships in a variety of ways: by reorganizing trade unions and political groups, by distributing the support given by international solidarity, by actively creating pressure for the release of political prisoners. They have also invented new methods in underground resistance. In Argentina and in Chile women have organized street demonstrations in protest against repression. In Santiago, Chile's capital city, the churches were taken over by women for their hunger strikes (May, 1978) which made a

6. Luis Vitale, *Historia y Sociologia de la Mujer Latino Americana,* (ed. Fontamara, Barcelona), 1981.

deep impression on the entire world as admirable examples of courage and determination in defying Pinochet's tyranny. Women's organizations have sent a letter to the United Nations, demanding that the Chilean government inform the U.N. about the prisoners who have "disappeared."

In Bolivia, women held a similar hunger strike at the beginning of 1978, which forced Banzer's government to decree a political amnesty. Thanks to it many political exiles were able to return home. Moema Wiezzer's dramatic publication of the testimony of Domitilia, a representative of the Bolivian mines, about the fight conducted by the Housewives Committees touched everyone.

Latin American women's participation in all fights against repressive regimes has taken such different forms as urban guerrillas (like the Tupamaros, in Uruguay), commented on by Ana Maria Araujo[7] and the overthrow of Somoza's dictatorship in Nicaragua and the putting into place of the Sandinista government, examined by Paz Espejo and Margaret Randall.[8]

Among the most striking forms women have invented to protest repression are the demonstrations regularly made by the Mothers of the Plaza de Mayo, in Buenos Aires. For many years they protested against the military terrorism responsible for the murder and "disappearance" of their husbands and sons, and they walked around the square with their heads covered with black material on which the name of the disappeared was printed. They called attention from all over the world and conquered the respect and admiration of millions of people for their silent but strong resistance. They were nominated for the Nobel Peace Prize.

In Brazil, mothers, sisters and daughters of political prisoners and refugees in exile conducted a long struggle in favor of amnesty. After years and years of despair and wandering around military prisons in

---

7. Ana Maria Araujo, *Tupamaras—Des femmes de l'Uruguay*, Ed. des femmes (Paris, 1980).

8. Paz Espejo, *Mujeres de Nicaragua* (Des femmes du Nicaragua), (Paris, 1980); Margaret Randall, *Todas estamos despiertas—Testimonios de la mujer nicaraguense hoy*, Siglo XXI Ed. (México, 1981).

an attempt to find out what had happened to their relatives, they won a battle when amnesty was declared.

Political Transition and Women's Participation

For some Latin American countries, a new period of so-called political opening has begun recently, and that is the case of Brazil. It means that the authoritarian regimes that have ruled the country for many years have undergone some important changes and there is a real possibility of bringing into politics large sectors of the population that have been marginalized until now.

On November 15, 1982, general elections took place in Brazil; these were for governors of states, federal and state representatives, local councillors and mayors. Millions of people had an opportunity to choose a political leader who would govern their state, after 18 years of an authoritarian regime. New political parties were organized to participate in that election after a change in the legislation was permitted in December 1979.

Compared to the elections of 1978, in the elections held in 1982 there were many more women candidates for different parties, as well as a number of women elected to parliamentary bodies at all levels. Besides, the feminist movement played a much more significant role in discussing political platforms and party programs. The feminist movement's slogans and demands were included in the campaigns of many candidates, and the possibility of using mass media, especially TV, to discuss feminist ideas most certainly helped to advertise the movement.

The fact that some feminists who are actively engaged in the movement and interested in defending women's needs have been elected should help get laws passed to improve the life conditions of women and to abolish remaining forms of discrimination. To a certain extent it may be taken as a guarantee for women's more active participation in the decision-making process.

Simultaneously, in Argentina, a broader participation of women in the definition of national politics may be expected, since the military junta has publicly asserted that general elections will take place and the date for such elections has even been announced. Feminist groups

117

created in that country in the last few years, as well as studies conducted on specific topics of women's social condition have made an important contribution to the role women can play in the period of transition to democracy. The existence of active political parties and the end of military government will certainly serve to bring more women into politics.

Nevertheless, some crucial questions will have to be solved. One of them is the disagreement that exists among the feminist groups concerning active engagement in political parties. Some consider that it is necessary to assure the "autonomy of the feminist movement" against parties' interests. In studying this particular question related to Brazil, I have argued[9] that the "political nature of the feminist movement should be oriented towards a *change* in the female's condition, so that she could be assured of equal rights. The institution that by its nature and character fights in the political arena is the party." So, it is essential that women join parties and be elected to parliament.

On the other hand, to convince women to join parties is not enough. It is absolutely necessary to strengthen the belief of some men who hold public office and are party leaders that bringing women into government is important. If this is important during the transition period, it is even more important after democracy has replaced an authoritarian regime. Otherwise, women's claims will hardly have a chance to succeed.

Women have most certainly earned the right to have effective participation in the period of transition that follows release from a strict authoritarian regime. In this respect, it is essential that political parties be progressive enough to understand the new and important contribution made by the feminist movement to women's role in society. It is crucial that leaders know how to establish a correct relationship between parties and movements, so that sexism and sex discrimination can really come to an end.

It is not an easy task, since feminists insist upon the absolute necessity of respecting the autonomy of their movement, i.e. they do not

---

9. Fanny Tabak, *Mulher e Política,* Ed. Paz e Terra, Rio de Janeiro, 1982, "A questão da autonomia do movimento feminista," Paper, ANPOCS, Rio, 1982.

want to have political parties interfere in their activities or to tell them what they should do. On the other hand, it is absolutely necessary that political parties learn how to incorporate women's specific needs into their political platforms. In present conditions in some of the Latin American countries it is crucial that women be brought into active political participation if a democratic regime hopes to come into existence. That means giving women an opportunity to take part in the decision-making process by discussing all the main issues that affect the future of our countries and asking women to put forward their hopes and expectations.

Periods of political transition are particularly difficult, as there is still the danger of going back to authoritarianism if the democratic forces are not strong enough to prevent it. One of the basic conditions for being successful in the implementation of a democratic rule is to get the support of the largest sectors of the population, which means women. The way to do it depends to a great extent on the flexibility of feminist groups and political organizations (not only parties). Can and will these groups convince women, from different classes, different ethnic origins and different religions to unite and fight for democracy?

6
PROLOGUE TO A FEMINIST CRITIQUE OF WAR AND POLITICS

Nancy C. M. Hartsock
Johns Hopkins University
Baltimore, Maryland

Prologue to a Feminist
Critique of War and Politics
Nancy C. M. Hartsock

For several thousand years, political power has been a gendered power in such a way that military capacity, civic personality, and masculinity have been coextensive. Here, by looking at a few ancient sources, I propose to begin though not complete an exploration of several related questions raised by this contention: how is the old adage, "war is simply politics by other means" connected with masculinity? Is the masculine political actor, the citizen warrior, capable of inhabiting a real democracy, that is, a world of equals who engage in rational consideration of the right actions for the community as a whole? Or is he more at home in agonistic and competitive settings where he can pursue the attainment of glory and honor?

Manhood and Military Valor

Masculinity and domination, virility and violence, have been frequently linked together. For example, in the literature on political power, many social scientists have remarked on the links between virility, potency, masculinity, and domination and noted that understandings of power appear "much sexier" than notions of influence or authority.[1] What is one to make of Henry Kissinger's telling but perhaps apocryphal remark, "power is the ultimate aphrodisiac?" Or

---

1. David Bell, *Power, Influence, and Authority* (New York: Oxford University Press, 1975), p. 8.

123

consider a 1915 poster titled "Why We Oppose Votes for Men." Among the reasons given are "because no really manly man wants to settle any question otherwise than by fighting about it," "because man's place is in the army," and "because if men should adopt peaceable methods women will no longer look up to them."[2]

The contemporary debate over whether to allow women in combat in the U.S. military also reveals these associations. Judith Stiehm has suggested that an important reason for the opposition to women in combat is that the role of warrior is the only role unique to men in modern society. Thus, in peacetime men lack a way to prove they are men. The inclusion of women would threaten the exclusiveness of the role of warrior and, therefore, men's identity.[3] Her argument is well illustrated by the comments of General Robert H. Barrow, current commander of the U.S. Marines:

> War is a man's work. Biological convergence on the battlefield [by which he must mean women serving in combat] would not only be dissatisfying in terms of what women could do, but it would be an enormous psychological distraction for the male, who wants to think that he's fighting for that woman somewhere behind, not up there in the same foxhole with him. It tramples the male ego. When you get right down to it, you have to protect the manliness of war.[4]

Not only gender is evoked in these statements, but some aspect of sexuality, or the erotic. Guns, we know, function as virility symbols.

---

2. Reprinted in *Radical America* XV, 1–2 (Spring, 1981), p. 147.

3. Judith Stiehm, "Implementation of Women's Integration into the U.S. Military Academies," a paper presented at the 1978 convention of the American Political Science Association, p. 12. She also notes that a frequent response to the suggestion that women become combatants is the statement, "it just isn't right," coupled with an inability to elaborate on this statement. She suggests that since women are frequently present on the battlefield, one must conclude not that men don't want them there, but that they don't want women on their side. (*Ibid.*, pp. 2, 7.) See also *Bring Me Men and Women: Mandated Change at the U.S. Air Force Academy* (Berkeley: University of California Press, 1981).

4. Michael Wright, "The New Marines: Life in the Pits," *This World, San Francisco Chronicle*, June 27, 1982.

And the peculiar terminology employed by the Chairman of the Joint Chiefs of Staff when he testified before the Senate Armed Services Committee provides an additional suggestion of the salience of such connections. He stated that "Deploying a new manned penetrator should be a top priority," and added that he believed we "must continue with the development of a manned penetrating aircraft to succeed the B-52."[5]

I will argue that these erotic aspects of civic personality should be centrally understood in terms of three general issues: 1) issues of relation with or connection to another, 2) issues of the role of sensuality or the body in political life, and 3) issues of creativity and generation. In each area, the masculine eroticism which forms a part of military valor is defined in such a way that connections with others take only the form of competition for dominance, the importance of the body is systematically denied, and creativity and generation are recast as a struggle to cancel death. As a result of these erotic dimensions, then, political power more generally takes the form of domination of all those outside the community, and within the community each citizen-warrior strives for mastery or preeminence. Finally, the citizen must attempt to dominate the bodily or sensual part of himself.

These links, moreover, are not accidental, but have been built into our ideals for public life from the beginning of Western political thought. Thus, the earliest Western notions about politics as these emerged in ancient Athens can provide a fruitful context in which to pursue these issues. These texts, the theoretical records of an all-male political community, directly contribute to our understanding of the gendered dimension of power through such things as their insistence that female existence (but not male) is defined by the body, and their presentation of mythic female forces as fundamental threats to the political community.[6]

The Greek understanding of politics and power rested more directly

---

5. Statement from the *New York Times,* January 29, 1981. E. V. Spelman called this to my attention.

6. See Elizabeth V. Spelman, "Woman and Body: Ancient and Contemporary Views," *Feminist Studies,* VIII, 1 (Spring 1982), and the discussion of the *Oresteia* below.

and explicitly than our own on the division between women and men, between the household, a private and apolitical space, and the *polis,* a public and political space. This division was, moreover, a division between a realm of necessity and a realm of freedom, a realm held to be characterized by inequality and a realm seen as populated by equals, a realm described as dominated by the body and a realm where the soul and intellect were held to be dominant. All of this both rested on and reinforced a profound misogyny. The result was a theorization of politics and political power as activities which occurred in a masculine arena characterized by freedom from necessary labor, dominance of intellect or soul, and equality among the participants, in which political power rested on heroic action defined by courage in war and courage in speech; in short, a world defined exclusively in masculine terms.[7]

To restate this in the language of *eros,* competition for dominance of others, the denial of the importance of the body, and a struggle to cancel death by achieving immortality were presented as the ideals for which the political actor, or citizen, should strive. Power in these ancient texts is intimately connected with (and indeed becomes an aspect of) masculinity in the person of the warrior–hero as he appears in the *Iliad.* He later takes the theoretical form of the good citizen who engages in rhetorical competition.

Yet, given the importance we still attribute to these ideals for political life, we should not conclude that attention to the nature of the Athenian political community holds only antiquarian interest. These ancient texts speak to our contemporary situation in important ways. They help us to understand some of the cultural roots of the commonplace associations of masculinity and domination. Moreover, we still treat these sources as profoundly important. Classicists such as James Redfield quite rightly hold that one of the reasons for our continuing fascination with the Greeks is that we are not so different from them. And scholars like Redfield who have interpreted them have often found Greek ideals not only admirable, but "uniquely true to the phenomena of experience." Nor is Redfield alone in arguing that the *Iliad*

---

7. It is worth reminding the reader that my use of the term "masculine" is intended to refer to the social rather than biological construction of gender.

more than any other poem, seems to "embody the mature understanding that a true man should have of his world."[8] To the extent that contemporary understandings of politics and power are rooted in these ideals, then, our own political life, too, must be understood to be structured by a masculine *eros* which links manhood with military valor, and virility with domination.

The Homeric Warrior–Hero: Face to Face with Death

The Homeric epics set the stage for the precarious community inhabited by heroes and later by citizens. In the *Iliad* the battlefield is the stage on which the action takes place. It is inhabited solely by men, and heroism is the supremely masculine role. Let us pursue this role as it appears in the character of Achilles.

As the best of the Achaeans, he carries in his person the clearest instance of the problems and possibilities of the hero. His honor defines his very being. The highest good for the warrior–hero is not a quiet conscience, but rather the enjoyment of public esteem, and through this esteem, immortality. Honor, or *time,* is central. Thus, Achilles can ask, "Why should I fight, if the good fighter receives no more *time* than the bad?"[9] The primacy of honor is memorialized both in Achilles' withdrawal from the battle over Troy because he feels his honor has been offended, and his choice between his "two destinies": he chooses to fight to win glory and immortality in the memory of men rather than return home to enjoy a "long life."[10]

The hero's honor (and thus his immortality in *kleos,* or poetry) is attained through the excellence of his *bie,* or force. And it is Achilles rather than Odysseus, the hero of *bie,* of force and potency rather than *metis,* or craft, who is the hero par excellence.[11] Moreover, the choice

---

8. James Redfield, *Nature and Culture in the Iliad: The Tragedy of Hector* (Chicago: University of Chicago Press, 1975), pp. xii, xiii.

9. See E. R. Dodds, *The Greeks and the Irrational* (Berkeley: University of California Press, 1951), pp. 17–18, citing *Iliad* IX, 315ff.

10. *Iliad* IX, 411–416, tr. Richard Lattimore (Chicago: University of Chicago Press, 1951).

11. Redfield, citing *Iliad* XVIII 105–106, p. 12.

of Achilles, the hero of force, must be recognized as not simply that of the poet; it represents centuries of cultural valuation of force over craft. The *Iliad* and the *Odyssey* were composed over time, and the fact that the *kleos* of Achilles at Troy preempted that of Odysseus (who was, after all, responsible for the victory at Troy through his craft) rested on a cultural choice of generations of listeners about who was the best hero.[12]

Both the centrality of force and the contradictory situation it creates for the hero are marked by the fact that the hero, through his force, or *bie*, confronts and overcomes death and mortality—ironically by means of his own death. His position is unique because while all men are born to die, the warrior's social role is defined by the fact that he must go to meet those who would kill him. Still, as one admirer of the warrior–hero has put it, "to die for something . . . is better than to die for nothing—and that is, after all, the alternative. In accepting death he shows himself searingly aware of it. The hero is in a sense rescued from mortality; he becomes godlike in status and immortal in memory."[13] The power of his achievement is indicated by the fact that he transcends the condition of both men and gods: "Men die, while the gods live forever; the hero, however, does both."[14] The hero gains his power and immortality through death and this feat cannot be matched even by the gods, since they cannot die. Heroism in combat, then, gives meaning to a world profoundly structured by death. Yet despite its tremendous cost, it remains a meaning only temporarily and uncertainly rescued from the meaninglessness introduced by death.[15]

The contradictory and conflicting requirements of the warrior–hero's situation were central to a larger series of conflicts and dualities in Greek understandings of the world. For them, *eris*, or strife, defined the human condition. Humans, they held, fell from a state

---

12. See Gregory Nagy, *The Best of the Achaeans* (Baltimore: Johns Hopkins Press, 1979), p. 41, on this point.

13. Redfield, p. 101. He cites the speech of Sarpedon, *Iliad* XII, 310–328.

14. Redfield, "Foreword," in Nagy, p. x.

15. Redfield, pp. 103, 126, 184, returns repeatedly to the problem of meaninglessness.

of primeval harmony into conflict, and their fate was to be a battle-ground for the opposing forces of these two worlds.[16] Thus, efforts to regain or reconstruct such a harmonious system were repeatedly made.

Yet at the same time, strife was built into the fundamental base of the community in the form of the definition of the community by rivalry and competition for honor. The nature of the fracture lines within the community are well illustrated by the quarrel between Achilles and Agamemnon which is the source of much of the action in the *Iliad*. The rivalry for the attainment of *time* is one in which one's *time* is only relative to that of the others in the system. Whatever one hero wins the other must lose.[17] Thus, the force which holds the community together—the collective practice of strife in war—is a central aspect of the community itself.[18]

Many Homer scholars have tended to see this constitution of the human condition by strife as not entirely negative. Thus, they have argued that only in its most negative form does it mean war. And some scholars such as Redfield even give some positive evaluation to war. On the battlefield, he argues, one has a tight-knit community of "those who are ready to die for one another."[19] Thus, he argues that although war in the beginning is an unhappy task, the prestige of the warrior leads in turn to war itself acquiring some positive value. Gregory Nagy treats war itself as more negative, but holds that competition, "that most fundamental aspect of most Hellenic institutions—including poetry itself," represents a more positive form of the same thing.[20] My own reading of the *Iliad* indicates that the heroes were far less willing to die for each other than for their own *kleos*. Achilles, after all, quits the war because his honor has been offended. And Odysseus is at one point abandoned by the other Greeks and left to make his own way

---

16. Redfield, "Foreword," p. xii.

17. Redfield, p. 33. Funeral games seem to be an exception to this pattern. *Ibid.*, p. 210. See also Nagy, p. 45 and M.I. Finley, *The World of Odysseus* (Baltimore: Penguin, 1979).

18. But see Redfield's very different argument on this point. p. 99.

19. *Ibid.*

20. Nagy, pp. 309–310.

out of the battlefield.[21] In addition, much of the combat described is, as Redfield admits, single combat.

Eris, or strife, is replicated at still another level within the being of each warrior–hero. Just as the warrior–hero faced the conflicts between himself and others in extreme form on the battlefield, so he faces this dualism in extreme form within his own being. It is perhaps the importance of public reputation that leads to the externalization of emotions. If to "lose face" is unbearable because it is to lose moral identity, how then can one explain actions one would be ashamed to acknowledge as one's own? In such circumstances, the society may allow individuals to project these feelings and actions onto some divine agency.[22] In Homer, for example, the emotions are seen as detached entities responsible for *ate,* a kind of temporary insanity or clouding of the normal consciousness in which the hero behaves in ways he cannot adequately explain. Within the person of the warrior–hero, then, a part is externalized and forms a dichotomy between the person himself and supernatural and alien forces which may overcome him from time to time.

This, then, is the "not-yet-citizen" who so importantly shaped both Athenian and our own views of politics. Now we must reformulate this account in terms which can more directly address the erotic dimensions of the warrior–hero's situation.

The Homeric Warrior–Hero: Remaking *Eros* as Death

Three distinct though not necessarily separate aspects of *eros* emerge in the psychological literature. The first is represented by Freud's definition of *eros* as "the desire to make one out of more than one."[23] This desire may take narrowly genital form, or may appear in other, sublimated forms. Freud suggests, and Marcuse agrees, that the inhibition of the direct aims of sexual impulses and their subjugation to the control of "higher psychical agencies which have subjected

---

21. *Iliad* XI, 404.

22. I owe this point to Dodds, Chapter I.

23. Sigmund Freud, *Civilization and Its Discontents,* translated by Joan Riviere (Garden City, New York: Doubleday, 1958), p. 57.

themselves to the reality principle," i.e., the repression of *eros,* is required for the development of civilization.[24]

The second aspect of *eros* turns on the role given to sensuality and bodily concerns in social life. Historically, various societies of Western civilization have found little place for this aspect of *eros* in public life.

Creativity and generation—whether intellectual creativity in philosophy and art, physical work on the natural world, or the generation of children through sexual relations—emerge as the third aspect of *eros.* Some psychologists have pointed to the pleasure in the "effortful achievement of purpose" as fundamental to what makes us human. They have suggested that only when these pleasures take pathological forms can sublimation (and the civilization on which it depends) occur.[25] Freud concurs at least to some extent when he argues that,

> No other technique of the conduct of life attaches the individual so firmly to reality as laying the emphasis on work; for his work at least gives him a secure place in a portion of reality, in the human community. The possibility it offers of displacing a large amount of libidinal components, whether narcissistic, aggressive, or even erotic, on to professional work and on to the human relations connected with it lends it a value by no means second to what it enjoys as something indispensable to the preservation and justification of existence in society . . . if it is a freely chosen one . . . it makes possible the use of existing inclinations . . . And yet, as a path to happiness, work is not highly prized by men.[26]

Eros, then, in both its narrowly genital forms and broader human meanings can be seen as involving first, the making of one out of more than one, or fusion with others; second, sensuality in a broad sense; and finally, creative activity. Yet this is only to describe the general issues covered by the concept of *eros.* We have not addressed the particular content each aspect of *eros* takes for the warrior–hero.

---

24. *Ibid.,* pp. 42–43.

25. Dorothy Dinnerstein, *The Mermaid and the Minotaur* (New York: Harper and Row, 1978), p. 140.

26. Freud, *Civilization,* p. 21.

In that highly masculine world populated by hostile and threatening others, each aspect of *eros* can only take negative forms. The desire for fusion with another, which could take the form of close and caring relationships, takes the form of a struggle for dominance. For the warrior–hero, relations with others take the paradigmatic form of the struggle for victory in battle, a struggle for dominance which requires the other's submission or even his death. The alternatives of victory versus death or dishonor mean that Hector and Achilles have no choices in common.

The second aspect of *eros,* too, sensuality and bodily concerns, could take the form of an acceptance of the body, its needs and its pleasures as worthy of attention. Yet here, too, *eros* takes negative form. The body and its needs—even for life itself—are held to be irrelevant. The warrior–hero must risk death if he is to gain a reputation for honor. And even his emotions are held to be not his own but products of detached entities responsible for creating temporary madness. Finally, creativity and generation, issues centering on life, are replaced for the warrior–hero by a fascination with death, a contradictory longing to cancel death by courting it. Ironically, it is physical death which most often provides the means for attaining undying fame. The rejection of life takes indirect form as well. The world in which heroic deeds are done exists in a space totally apart from daily life activity. To gain and preserve his honor the warrior–hero must show himself to be "above" concerns of necessity and daily life.

The Homeric warrior–hero, then, contained within his person and situation many of the contradictory forces which would take attenuated form in the life of the Athenian citizen and, later, the philosopher. But while the citizen, the philosopher, and the hero are similar, they are not one and the same. The transition from the tribal or clan-based world portrayed in the Homeric poems to the world of the *polis* is marked in poetic and mythological terms by the *Oresteia* of Aeschylus in the fifth century B.C., a series of plays which can be most instructive for our purposes.

The Mythic Founding of the *Polis*

The transition required was a great one, from what was basically a stratified tribal society to a settled, class-divided community, from an oral culture to a written one. These plays can be read as fifth century representations of a mythic founding of the *polis* and (in the process) an important development of Western understandings of politics and power. This reading is not unique to me. Both Simone de Beauvoir and Kate Millett have seen these plays as the mythic rendering of a patriarchal takeover.[27] George Thomson, from a Marxist perspective, has seen them as a mythic account of the beginnings of Greek democracy, which, based as it was on a system of private property, required the subjection of women.[28]

The *Oresteia* marks a second and related important transition as well, a transition in the definition of *eros*. Gender has become implicated in the negative forms of *eros* we discovered at work in the world of the warrior–hero. Most fundamentally, in these plays, the establishment of the *polis* takes place through a process of domesticating and subordinating dangerous and threatening female forces which surround what is to become the all-male political community, forces whose symbolic sources are the earth and the night, forces seen as deeply connected with fertility, sexuality, and reproduction. Thus, the plays indicate that the Furies, the avengers of matricide from the darkness beneath the earth, must be persuaded to accept a role in Athens— not a role which has to do with the masculine concerns of war, politics, and the search for immortality, but rather a role which gives them power over "mortal" ways and daily life. (It is worth noting as well the ways in which these former realms are open to virgins, if not women.)

At the simplest level, the *Oresteia* is a tale of family vengeance: a

27. Simone de Beauvoir, *The Second Sex*, translated by H. M. Parshley (New York: Knopf, 1953), p. 73; Kate Millet, *Sexual Politics* (Garden City, New York: Doubleday, 1970), pp. 111–115.

28. George Thomson suggests that this consequence was recognized even by contemporaries of Aeschylus; both Aristophanes and Plato saw that the abolition of private property would involve the emancipation of women. See Slater, *The Glory of Hera* (Boston: Beacon Press, 1971), pp. 161–193; Thomson, *Aeschylus and Athens* (London: Lawrence & Wishart, 1941), p. 288.

son kills his mother who has killed his father who in turn has killed his sister. The son is hounded by the Furies, avengers of matricide, but rescued by the intervention of Apollo and directed to Athens. There Athena, the virgin goddess, calls the Athenian jurors into session to hear his case. What is at issue is who is guilty of the worst crime, and in resolving this issue the plays become an opposition of male and female forces—Apollo, Orestes, and Athena on one side, and Clytemnestra and the Furies on the other.

Yet the plays are more than this. Their significance is marked by the fact that Greek theater served not simply a theatrical but a ritual purpose. Myths were rewritten as plays. And in the rewriting many of the concerns of fifth and fourth century Athens were projected into the plays. The plays, then, served a communal purpose in which contemporary problems were "doubly displaced"—from the present to the past, and from public world to the household—especially the royal household of an ancient king where the most disruptive "public" actors were women.[29]

Let us look more directly at the presentation of the three aspects of *eros* in the plays and the ways *eros* has acquired both gender and gender-specific duality. Strife fundamentally defines the relations of the characters in the plays, a strife brought about by dangerous and disorderly female forces. These unruly females threaten the fragile masculine community in several ways. One can see some of these threats in the figure of Clytemnestra. She functions in the plays as the representative of the older, clan-based order which operated on the ethic of the blood vendetta. As such she is not only out of place in the new world of law where decisions are made by the jury, but is also an indication of how disruptive the old ways may now be. And even within the context of the clan system, the fact that she has killed her husband indicates that a woman's responses to provocation can be expected to exceed the proper (here read masculine) response, and lead to disequilibrium. The figure of Clytemnestra holds yet another threat to the political community. She is a sexual creature who has demon-

---

29. The term "double displacement" is Jack Winkler's, from a presentation to the Stanford University Feminist Studies Seminar, Fall, 1982.

strated her ability to act on her own by taking a lover while her husband was away.

The dangers female forces present to the political community appear in slightly different form in the case of the Furies. They appear as elements of the archaic, "old religion," characterized as primitive, lawless, regressive, and tied to the forces of earth and nature, while the male, "bright Apollo," is seen as leading toward the future—law abiding, orderly, and by implication part of the world of reason. Because of the danger the female presents to the male world, the plays can be read as a statement of the importance fifth century Athenians gave to domesticating the forces of disorder. Failing this domestication, they feared, the male community could not survive.

The *polis* is mythically founded on the new, explicitly patriarchal religion of the Olympian Gods: the meaning of the transition to this new religion is made clear in the images of the opposition of light to darkness, Apollo to the Furies. The Athenian jury which decides Orestes' fate is the institution which replaces the blood feud. The conflict between Orestes and Clytemnestra, the Furies and Apollo, and by implication between Zeus and the Moirae, can be seen as a poetic restatement of the real historical process of moving from tribe to state.[30]

More is involved, however, than the transition from tribe to class society. The end of the plays, with the Furies dutifully taking their place beneath the city, makes it clear that the patriarchal state has now taken control of the female *eros* they represent. In addition, the political community is now defined by a masculine *eros* which operates through the double means of the Athenian jury, a group of the wisest citizens (the future Council of the Areopagus), and Athena, a benevolent female figure without whose intervention Orestes (and by implication even Apollo) could not have won the trial.

The defining presence of a masculine *eros* reminiscent of the warrior–hero is evidenced by the presentation of the relation to the other parties as a deep-going conflict, and of the female figures as both hostile and powerful, so powerful that even a man aided by a god can-

30. Thomson argues that this is the beginning of the reign of law. I would argue that it represents a mythic representation of a change in the mode of production—from tribal society to a class state. See Thomson, p. 289.

not control them. Even together, they require the aid of yet another female figure, a virgin goddess.[31]

The concluding substitution of this less sexual, less earthy, and less fertile *eros* is prefigured in the person of Athena herself. In contrast to Clytemnestra and the Furies, Athena's distance from sexuality, fertility, and reproduction is extreme. She is a virgin, yet she is even less a sexual and female being than other virgin goddesses because her birth itself was extraordinary; she sprang not even from the body of a god but from his head.[32]

Let us look more closely at the shifts in the content of the masculine *eros* evidenced in these plays. The first aspect of *eros*, fusion or relation with another, continues to take forms requiring the subordination of one party to the other. But where for the Homeric warrior–hero this relation took the form of a struggle for the death of the other, now the struggle is moderated: in order to prevent the Furies from destroying the male community, they must be persuaded to accept a subordinate role. One might see this as well as evidence that even at the level of myth-making, the Greeks recognized that they could ignore neither their own need for continuance nor the forces of life represented by these female figures, however dangerous or disorderly their presence might be for men.

Similar changes occurred in terms of the second aspect of *eros*, the aspect related to the place of sensuality and the body. The control of the disorderly, earthy, and fertile female forces was allied with a reinforcement of the necessity for the mind to rule the body, reason to rule

---

31. Slater's discussion suggested this point. Slater cites Erich Neuman, *The Great Mother* (Princeton: Princeton University Press, 1963), p. 215, as an example of the powerlessness and fragility of male forces. Perseus is barely able to kill the Medusa with two gods helping, magic implements, a sleeping enemy, and a goddess guiding his hand. This buttressing reflects for Slater the brittleness of masculine self-confidence among the Greeks. (Slater, "The Greek Family in History and Myth," *Arethusa* VII, (Spring 1974), p. 40).

32. *Oresteia*, translated by Philip Villacot (Baltimore: Penguin Books, 1956), p. 169. Can one say that these dual types of female figures in some way anticipate the opposition between virgin and whore in more contemporary contexts?

the senses. But whereas the warrior–hero externalized his own emotions, with the founding of the *polis* there is a shift to an insistence simply that the appetites be suppressed and denied in favor of the rule of reason. Freud approvingly recognized the importance of this shift when he noted that the founding of the *polis,* especially the turning from mother to father, "signifies a victory of intellectuality over the senses." Thus, he appears to agree with Aeschylus and those who preserved these plays that civilization itself depends on controlling the (female) forces of disorder within the individual.[33] The *Oresteia,* then, can be read as an account of the establishment of a harmonious and unitary political whole, in which the different parts take their proper place, and in which female is subordinate to male, body to soul, and emotion to reason.

The shifts in the third aspect of *eros,* generation and creativity, are most dramatically expressed in Apollo's defense of Orestes, since here Apollo argues that only the male and not the female is the true source of new life. The mother, he claims, is not the real parent, but rather a "nurse who tends the growth of the young seed planted by its true parent, the male."[34] So "if fate spares the child, she keeps it as one might keep for some friend a growing plant."[35] Thus, rather than the fascination with death and the search for immortality in the memories of man, Apollo's speech represents a much more literal claiming of female fertility for the male.

---

33. Sigmund Freud, *Moses and Monotheism* (n. p. : n. d.), p. 145, cited in Froma Zeitlin, "The Dynamics of Misogyny: Myth and Myth-Making in the *Oresteia,*" *Arethusa* XI, 1–2 (Spring and Fall, 1978). Zeitlin also presents a useful tabulation of the male/female polarization in Greek thought—a polarization which put reason and the appetites in opposition to each other, and which associated reason with the male, and appetites with the female and which required that the stronger of the two opposing forces should control.

34. *Oresteian Trilogy* (Penguin), p. 169.

35. This is, of course, a restatement of the influential Pythagorean view, and also of the Aristotelian view. See Thomson, *Aeschylus and Athens,* p. 288; Marilyn Horowitz, "Aristotle and Woman," in *Journal of the History of Biology,* vol. IX, no. 2, Fall 1976, p. 194, on the plant analogy, and pp. 198–202 on the vision of the female as a mutilated male.

In such a reading, the *Oresteia* can be seen as describing a shift, though not a transformation, in each aspect of eros. Thus, rather than take revenge on one's enemies by killing them, opponents take part in rhetorical competition before the Athenian jury. Rather than risking the death of the body in combat and externalizing the emotions, the *Oresteia* suggests that the subordination of bodily appetites and sexuality to the rule of reason is sufficient.

The Disembodiment of the Citizen in Philosophy

These shifts, along with an increasingly explicit characterization of *eros* in gendered terms, appear in much more systematic form in the corpus of Platonic philosophy. The *Symposium* is particularly valuable in describing the creation of a ritualized and disembodied *eros* between masculine citizens. In this dialogue Plato is less involved in the Aeschylean (and later Aristotelian) project of claiming female fertility for the male than attempting to move *eros* away from the disorderly realm of the female and the physical and toward reason, away from bodily concerns and toward those of the soul (ultimately toward the divine). Only when it is cleansed of enough of its bodily impurities and its associations with the female can *eros* take its place as an honorable tie among citizens.

The structure of the dialogue itself replicates the transition from warrior–hero to citizen–philosopher and indicates the shifting but continuing association of manliness both with the negative forms of *eros* we have described, and with efforts to subjugate what are conceived of as female forces.

Phaedrus and Pausanius begin the discussion—both describing love as a kind of possession by an alien invader. In addition, they stress the importance of reputation—a concern clearly in tune with the values of the ancient heroes. Phaedrus stresses the links between *eros* and military virtue, or courage in battle. He argues, for example, that the lover would be unable to bear that his beloved should find him in an inglorious act. He turns directly to the military possibilities in this, and suggests that if a city or army were composed of none but lovers and beloved, they might well conquer the world. "For the lover would

138

rather any one than his beloved should see him leave the ranks or throw away his arms in flight."[36]

He makes explicit the relation of *eros* and the warrior–hero when he argues that Homer's statement that some god "breathed might" into one of the heroes is in reality a reference to the power of love in the heart of the lover. Moreover, Phaedrus is impressed not only with the willingness of the lover to die for the beloved, but also with his wish to avenge him. Conflict and the struggle for dominance, then, whether in the form of wishing to distinguish oneself in the eyes of the beloved by dominating others or wishing to destroy others for vengeance are central to the *eros* of the masculine citizen.

Pausanius then presents the appearance of disagreeing (in order to distinguish himself) but carries forward the argument Phaedrus had begun. His contribution focuses on the dualism of mind and body and the proper ordering of the two in the worthy lover, an ordering which rejects sensuality in favor of submission only in search of wisdom or other virtue. Pausanius suggests that there are two sorts of love, the one represented by the heavenly and the other by a common Aphrodite. Common love, the love that inferior men feel, works at random, and thus inferior men "love firstly women as well as boys; next when they love, they love bodies rather than souls."[37]

Common Aphrodite had a share of both male and female in her birth, and it is the share of the female which is responsible for the sensual, bodily orientation of this kind of love. The other love, and the higher goddess, had no share of the female but only the male. She is the elder and does not inspire violent passions. Those inspired by this goddess feel affection for boys who have shown signs of intelligence (signs which usually appear with the first growth of beard.)[38]

Pausanius' argument essentially amounts to a claim that the *eros* appropriate to the political actor must reject the body in favor of the soul, and must reject the material and not-lasting in favor of higher things.

---

36. *Symposium,* translated by Michael Joyce, 179:a.

37. *Ibid.,* 180b–182c. The association of the two was also shared by Aristotle. See his discussion of human reproduction in *De Generatione Animalium.*

38. *Ibid.,* 181d.

But because of the overlay of gender, the *eros* of the masculine political actor must, most fundamentally, reject the female.

The *Symposium* progresses through Eryximachus' and Aristophanes' development of themes of harmonization, reconciliation, and the
search for fusion with another, which form the basis for the sublimation and final disembodiment of *eros*. Aristophanes, once again claiming to take the argument in a different direction, turns the theme of
harmonization into an argument about the dichotomous nature of a
gendered *eros*.

He develops the idea of harmony (mediation and reconciliation)
through his story of the original three human sexes. The original male,
female, and mixed-sex creatures, each now sliced in half by Zeus, "attempt to reintegrate our former nature, to make two into one, and to
bridge the gulf between one human being and another." This fusion is
a weak reflection of the dream of being a single and harmonious
whole with one's beloved.[39] Yet the fusion itself carries the gender hierarchy: only the original male creatures are capable of the highest
love.

Agathon and Socrates/Diotima move the consideration of *eros* toward the disembodied love of truth or wisdom. Agathon contributes
an argument that love, however heroic, is a poet versed in all creative
arts.[40] It is, he argues, longing, desire, and lack which have led to the
development of all the arts. Socrates carries the case still further. *Eros*
is a mediator between mortal and immortal. He can fulfill this role
through his longing for the beautiful—a longing apparent in all the
arts, because the longing for the beautiful and the good, is, as well, a
longing for immortality.[41] Reproduction, creativity and generation,
then, the third aspect of *eros*, take only the disembodied form of the
search for immortality.

The material interactions with real objects involved in creative
physical work are rejected in favor of a longing for immortality, a desire to cancel death. Significantly Diotima states that this longing for
immortality takes the forms both of procreation and a desire for "eter-

39. *Ibid.*, 192e.
40. *Ibid.*, 196d.
41. *Ibid.*, 207a. See also 204c–205d.

nal mention in the deathless role of fame."[42] "For the sake of fame they will dare greater dangers, even, than for their children; they are ready to spend their money like water and to wear their fingers to the bone, and, if it comes to that, to die." Moreover, she adds, those who hope for this endless fame are more noble than others because they are "in love with the eternal."[43] Only some men, however, are capable of achieving this latter kind of immortality. Here the discussion once again supports the hierarchical and gendered vision of male and female, soul and body, reason and appetite.

The vision of a gendered *eros* takes most striking form in the argument that all men are pregnant in both body and soul. Those who are pregnant in body turn to women, and raise a family, in the hope that they are securing immortality, memory and happiness. In contrast those who are pregnant in soul conceive and bear such things as wisdom and all her sister virtues. This group by attaching themselves to others (beautiful in both body and soul) can bear beautiful and immortal children; and as Socrates/Diotima says, "who would not prefer such fatherhood to merely human propagation, if he stopped to think of Homer, and Hesiod, and all the greatest of our poets? Who would not envy them their immortal progeny, their claim on the admiration of posterity?"[44] The real activity of reproduction and women's pregnancy is thus replaced by the mental activity of men achieving wisdom and immortality. The citizen has become disembodied.

Procreation involves only the spirit; the flesh is irrelevant.

Let us review what has happened to each aspect of *eros* in this discussion. The *Symposium* marks the codification of the shifts we noted in the *Oresteia*. Yet once again it is evident that despite some changes, because the political community remained deeply structured by masculinity, the fundamental concerns remained unchanged. The speeches of the *Symposium* indicate that gender as a metaphor for the issues raised by each aspect of *eros* has come to be ubiquitous. Yet now the female is treated less as dangerous and disorderly than simply pitiable.

---

42. *Ibid.,* 208c.
43. *Ibid.,* 208e.
44. *Ibid.,* 209d.

Fusion or community with another continues to operate through the effort to subordinate and control the other. But whereas for the warrior–hero this effort took the form of combat, for the masculine citizen a ritualized rhetorical competition (such as takes place in the *Symposium*) can substitute. Loathing for the body and a denial of its needs no longer requires the disregard for the body to be demonstrated by risking death. Instead, the good citizen must force his reason to rule over violent passions and sublimate sensual and bodily love into the love of truth or wisdom, a translation, perhaps of sexuality into philosophy. Creativity and generation, too, continue to take negative form. But Plato retheorizes the effort to achieve immortality by dying a glorious death in terms more closely connected to reproduction.

The gaining of immortality no longer requires one's literal death, nor is the begetting of children as literally biological as it was in the *Oresteia*. Now, rather than claim to "really," though not obviously, producing the child borne by the woman, men in association with other men claim to have taken over the pregnancy too! Yet this time it is a disembodied pregnancy which produces only disembodied children, whose most important purpose is to ensure the man's immortality.[45] The effort to cancel death, thus, now focuses more directly on efforts to associate reproduction with manliness.

The Nature of the Political Community

The *eros* of the community lies at the heart of its life as a community; the forms taken by *eros* indicate the fundamental structure of the community itself. As presented in theoretical form the ancient political community is both fragile and unsatisfactory. The community is fragile in part because the warrior–hero (and his citizen successor) is a brittle and fragile creature, not only threatened on all sides by those against whom he fights, but also in danger from a female world. From this perspective, the *polis* represents the community built to protect

---

45. See Mary O'Brien's very interesting discussion of the significance of second birth in political ideology, *The Politics of Reproduction* (Boston: Routledge and Kegan, 1981).

the warrior–heroes and to subjugate these threats—a community based on and defined by its maleness. It segregates the female forces—both material and figurative—and also splits off the female forces within each man represented by the bodily and appetitive parts of their humanness.

The forces which hold this fragile community together are the same as those which threaten to destroy it. The *eros* which holds it together may break it apart (as in the *Iliad*) unless it is disembodied and sublimated; and competition for dominance must be ritualized lest it become the all-out war of each against all. The *polis* both carried on the heroic ideal in which the virtues of citizenship required valor in battle in wartime and courage in rhetorical competition in peacetime, and attempted to reconcile and ritualize the conflicts to which this gave rise.

The fundamental dualism of the Homeric poems continued to structure political life. Fame and honor and glory in both situations were to be gained at the price of another losing *his* fame, honor, and glory.[46] The continued importance of military imagery in the political vocabulary is striking. The centrally important terms of commendation for the Athenians were *arete* and *agathos*. Both were terms which commended military bravery and success in war. To be *agathos* is above all to be independent of the constraint of another—due, it is implied, to one's military success. As daily life moved away from the battlefield, the nature of the combat among citizens changed but retained its character of competition or contest, the object of which was to achieve as much recognition as possible especially among the group of fellow citizens who could be considered contestants in the same game.[47]

One can now begin to see some of the possible significance of both the association of reason with the male and of the particular Platonic

46. Slater notes that one is struck repeatedly by the zero-sum nature of Athenian competition; the "twin delicacies of daily life were to achieve revenge and to arouse envy." See Slater, "The Greek Family in History and Myth," pp. 25, 35–36. See also Alvin Gouldner, *Enter Plato* (New York: Basic Books, 1965), pp. 48–50.

47. Gouldner, *Enter Plato,* pp. 48–53 documents this feature of Greek life.

(and to a lesser extent Aristotelian) conception of reason. Plato viewed human beings as materials the planner must work against, rather than with—materials on which the planner must impose himself, since they are disorderly and chaotic.[48] When Plato constructs a just community in the *Republic,* he does so according to the dictates of reason—a reason which is associated with the need to control and master the world, to dominate natural objects and bend them to human will. The community he creates is both ordered and perfect. Yet the description of the process of degeneration (significantly a degeneration set in motion by women) in Book VIII of the *Republic* makes it clear that even the perfect community established in the best possible way has tendencies toward disorder.

One can note as well that for Plato order itself is equated with hierarchy. Even Plato's conception of reason itself is infected with the essential hierarchical quality of his outlook. Reason for him is not simply another human faculty: it is the master of all of them, the only one with a legitimate claim to command. Reason can be either the master of the passions or their slave: domination or submission is the only possible choice in the relationship.

In this world in which reason takes the form of a combative agent of domination, Plato mistrusts the senses and suggests that they may corrupt reason and virtue both in the city and in the individual. The warrior and guardian classes must exercise the cardinal virtues: courage, temperance, justice, and wisdom.[49] To do so, the citizen must be free of the necessity to labor. Indeed, a city based on necessity alone is described as a city of pigs.[50] One might suggest that the citizen, in order to exercise the cardinal virtues must be free of the demands of the body in order to allow his soul, or rational part, to rule. This, after all, is one of the points of the massive education of the senses in the *Re-*

---

48. Gouldner makes this point.

49. *Republic* IV, 427e–432d.

50. See, for a different view of the significance of the city of pigs imagery, Arlene W. Saxonhouse, "Comedy in Callipolis: Animal Imagery in the *Republic,*" in *The American Political Science Review,* VXXII, No. 3 (September 1978), pp. 888–901.

public where music and exercise are to be used along with other techniques to ensure the rule of reason in the lives of the guardian class.[51]

The fear that the material or the necessary will contaminate the divine shows clearly in Plato's refusal to allow the guardian class to have any property other than what is absolutely necessary, and his insistence that they live in common and share possessions. Were they to get land, they would become householders and farmers instead of guardians. That is, they would have become contaminated by the realm of necessity.

It is a fascinating commentary on the Greek view of the relative strength of the soul and body that the soul seems to have no chance of ruling if necessary labor or property or any aspect of the realm of necessity and daily life intrudes into the citizen's life. The only way to protect the soul of the citizen is to wall it off as much as possible from necessity, and thus from the female.

As to the subduing of inner as well as external nature foreshadowed in the *Oresteia*, Plato is explicit about the proper ordering of the human soul. Indeed, the only respect Socrates gives what might be termed the irrational side of his own soul occurs in his account of his *daemon*. And Socrates externalizes this aspect of his being by calling it a *daemon*. He never acknowledges it as a part of himself, and, in part due to this refusal, never accepts the passions and appetites of individuals as creative, energetic, and fundamentally enriching aspects of the human character.[52] In this of course he is part of the tradition which goes back at least as far as Homer's invocation of the madness of *ate* as an explanation for the actions of the heroes.

The basic polarity in Plato's view of social thought and action, then, is the opposition of emotional or appetitive to rational behavior. Plato

---

51. Although Plato includes women in his guardian class, they are detached from the world of necessity and nature. They participate not as females but as asexual beings. See O'Brien's cogent argument on this point in *The Politics of Reproduction*.

52. See, for example, the passage in the *Republic* where he says that the soul not ruled by reason would be unable to act because the passions would oppose it at every turn. See Gouldner, *Enter Plato*, p. 337. But see especially the role of the *daemon* in the *Apology, Crito,* and *Phaedo*.

is seeking to assimilate the rational and divine—in part through the role both have in the mastery of nature (both external and internal nature). This serves to heighten the opposition between the rational and the appetitive. The rational faculty arranges things and, by naming, imposes order on the world. The divine then becomes pure mind, and as a result, the excellent citizen is disembodied.

The community of competitors threatens to destroy itself—to degenerate into the war of each against all—unless the competition for dominance is ritualized and regulated. *Eros* too could take a destructive form, but it can also serve to protect the community.[53] *Eros* can help to ritualize the competition and to direct it away from dangerous competitions. The community must incorporate *eros,* including its explicitly sexual dimensions, to develop ways for the many to become one. It accomplishes this through the *eros* of male citizens for each other.[54] There is, of course, a contradiction between competition as their way of life on the one hand and the maintenance of the community through their *eros* for each other on the other, a conflict which is never satisfactorily resolved and becomes a contributing factor to the fragility of the political community.

The community as a whole, the *polis,* exists for the purpose of, or in Aristotle's terms, has as its end, the arranging of competition among its citizens to show that they are worth loving or (the same thing within the Athenian context) to show that they are worth dominating. That is, the citizen–warrior must show that a victory over him is significant enough to make his vanquisher preeminent among citizens, a victory which will mean the achievement of honor and glory.

The political community is an exclusively male community, one in which power and sexuality are intertwined, a community in which the exercise of political power involves rule over those who are originally presumed to be equal, over those who can show they are worth loving, over those who might be able to turn the tables. In this community, only through dominating those worth dominating can one achieve glory and honor. Thus, the political world of equals shows it-

---

53. See, for example, the first half of *Phaedrus.*

54. The institution of Greek homosexuality has been usefully discussed by Kenneth J. Dover in *Greek Homosexuality* (New York: Vintage Books, 1978).

self to be unstable, a world which will quickly become a world of un-equals.

The point I have attempted to make is that *eros* and power are deeply connected, and when *eros* takes negative, masculine forms which point toward death rather than life, the community as a whole will be structured by those dynamics. The political community which rests on negative forms of *eros* can now be seen to be structured by a deep and through-going hostility; its participants are not simply strangers to each other but enemies who compete for dominance. In this community, the search for reciprocal fusion with another takes the essential form of the search for the conquest of the other's will. Moreover, in the competition for mastery the one competitor could only gain what the other lost. Yet each combatant needs the other: recognition grows from the death struggle (or rhetorical competition) with a worthy opponent. At the same time, however, the death of the other, especially his heroic death, negates the recognition of the power of the victor, and his humiliation or dishonor makes him unfit to confer recognition on the prowess of the victor. Thus, the need for recognition of one's mastery in competition carries with it a number of contradictory requirements.[55]

The second aspect of *eros,* sensuality and bodily concerns, takes the negative form of the denial of the importance of the body and of mortality. The denial of mortality takes the forms of valuing the risking of

---

55. Interestingly, the public world constructed by the *eros* of citizen-warriors is more overtly and directly a setting for the playing out of relations of domination and submission. The erotic dimension of power is less overlaid than other aspects of power by an ideology which attempts to present coercion as choice, or inequality as equality. Perhaps this is because neither the domination of women by men (whether sexually or otherwise) nor the fact that erotic relations took forms of domination/submission has been open to question until very recently. In contrast, the commitment to human equality characteristic of political theorists from the 16th century on was integral to the generation of accounts of social relations which took human freedom and equality as unquestioned givens, and proceeded to give accounts of social life which argued that visible relations of inequality and bondage were illusory.

physical death in favor of legendary immortality, giving great weight to the organizing powers of reason rather than real work in the material world, and subjugation of the sensual and appetitive parts of the soul to the rational aspect—the disembodying of the good citizen.

The third aspect of *eros,* too, creativity and generation, in these ancient sources takes the form of a rejection of the importance of any creative work other than disembodied mental activity and a devaluing of the real children born to women in favor of the children which can be born to the minds of men not contaminated by the concerns of necessity or the body.

The result is that power appears as domination not only of others but of parts of oneself—domination both internal and external, and the community itself rests on dualism and contradiction. Power is domination of those outside the community. It requires an attempt to dominate materiality, women, slaves, and barbarians. Second, within the community, each citizen must strive for mastery or preeminence. And third, it requires the attempt to dominate the appetitive and irrational part of the self. The fear of and contempt for the bodily, the irrational, the appetitive, and ultimately, the female are all part of the same pattern. These then are the forms of *eros* central to the ancient texts which still influence our thinking about politics.

What emerges from all this is an understanding of the political community which rests on dualism and contradiction, in which the two realms are in opposition and in which the higher world depends on the lower world. Just as in the individual the higher part should rule the lower part, so too in the community, the best should rule. But in the literal way the *Republic* takes the analogy of the nature of the individual to the community, the existence of the rules (soul, reasoning part) depends on the survival of the ruled (or body), and yet can only be distorted and corrupted by the demands of the ruled.

The contradictory nature of the community emerges in several areas. First, the *eros* of the citizens which holds the community together is constantly threatened by their competition with each other. Each man's effort to distinguish himself at someone else's expense creates a situation in which the existence of the community is constantly threatened. The *polis* could disintegrate into a battlefield. Even the *eros* of citizens is invaded by this competition: each man wishes to distinguish himself in the eyes of his beloved, wishes to dominate others for the sake of the beloved, thereby showing himself capable of taking only the most worthy as lover.

Second, the realm of politics, the public realm, both depends on and exists only in opposition to the private realm, that is, the household. One can only be a citizen by being the head of a household. Third, the realm of freedom and leisure inhabited by citizens depends on the existence of a realm of necessity populated by women, slaves, and laborers—but defined in essence by its female nature. Fourth, there is an opposition between an unstable realm in which political rule is possible—rule over formal equals where there is a constant possibility of changing from ruler to ruled—and a stable private realm in which the ruler's dominance can never be changed by the ruled. The citizen must be involved in this realm of unequals to quality for entering the public realm.

Conclusion

Let us return to the issues broached at the outset of this paper. The masculine political actor as he appears in these ancient texts is indeed most at home in agonistic and competitive settings, whether the battlefield or the *agora*, where he can pursue the attainment of glory, honor, and immortality in the memory of men. The calm and rational consideration of the best actions for the community as a whole are of less concern to him than his own status within it. Rather than war being politics by other means, political action as it appears in these texts is simply war by other means. And through this war, citizens attain and celebrate manhood.

For Achilles and Hector, there could be no complete manhood without war. Despite the moderating of the conflict in the Athenian *polis,* General Barrow's remarks make it clear that similar views are still extant. Yet today, when the destructive power of our weapons could destroy life on earth, we cannot defend current military practices on the grounds put forward by General Barrow: the need to protect the male ego. We must break the linkage of masculinity with both military capacity and civic personality. We must shift the *eros* of the political community from its negative, masculine forms to more positive forms which do not require the rejection of the female. The admission of women to the political community as full participants—including fully shared civil and military responsibilities—would be an important step both toward breaking these links and forging more satisfactory alternatives. Perhaps then, we might be able to construct a more complete democracy.

7
DESPOTISM AND CIVIL SOCIETY: THE LIMITS OF PATRIARCHAL CITIZENSHIP

Anna Yeatman
Flinders University
Bedford Park, South Australia

Despotism and Civil Society: The Limits of Patriarchal Citizenship
Anna Yeatman

Introduction

C.B. Macpherson argued that the kind of individuality presupposed in the conception of civil society that social contract theorists like Hobbes and Locke elaborated was one that expressed itself in capitalism's self-seeking.[1] That is, the individual was determined by a competitive and possessive individualism, and this self-seeking entailed the capitalist relation of class domination. This argument has become an orthodoxy in contemporary social and political theory. Its implication is that capitalism and civil society are mutually determined. In this paper, I will examine anew the particular kind of individuality civil society entails, and inquire whether there may be some necessary relation between civil society and a gender division of labor. If this turns out to be the case, and if we accept C.B. Macpherson's thesis, there would be a connection between civil society, capitalism, and a gender division of labor as well.

Here, however, I will confine myself to the issue of whether there is an intrinsic connection between civil society and gender domination. I propose such a connection: that the individual of civil society is both a masculine, and a patriarchal individual. Accordingly, the universal-

---

1. See C.B. Macpherson, *The Political Theory of Possessive Individualism: Hobbes to Locke* (London: Oxford University Press, 1962).

ity of this type of individuality should be qualified in two crucial respects.

In the first part of this paper, I argue that civil society presupposes, or requires, a gender division of labor. To do so I employ an "ideal-type" of civil society based on a synthetic analysis of that concept as developed by Hobbes, Locke, Montesquieu, Rousseau and Hegel.[2] In this section I may appear to derive gender domination from the requirements of civil society; it is important to point out, however, that the inverse could be argued in an equally persuasive manner. That is, it could be argued that gender domination produces the kind of (masculine) individuality that expresses itself in possessive individualism and in instrumental rationality.[3] My thesis, then, proposes that civil society and gender domination are mutually required terms of the same structure.

In the second part of this paper, I elaborate and illustrate the analytic section with a discussion of Montesquieu's description of domestic despotism as it appears in *The Persian Letters.* Among the classical exponents of the idea of civil society, Montesquieu is the only one to give extended consideration to the relationship between the public and domestic domains within a particular social type. He is also the only one to suggest that this relationship (and the domains themselves) is relative to each social type and, thus, is social in character. Montesquieu's analysis of domestic despotism is illuminating precisely because he conceives the gender division of labor as a social relation of domination, not as natural and not as given.

I conclude this essay with some remarks concerning the implications of the patriarchal determination of civil society for the nature of its citizenship, and for the extension of its citizenship to women. Curiously enough, for reasons I will show, membership in civil society is open in formal terms to women. Still, this does not qualify the basis for

---

2. See my doctoral dissertation "The Classical Theory of Civil Society: an Analytic Critique," State University of New York at Binghamton, 1980.

3. See e.g., Jessica Benjamin's analysis in "The Bonds of Love: Rational Violence and Erotic Domination," *Feminist Studies,* 6:1 (Spring, 1980), 144–175.

gender domination, and for the dependence of civil society on domestic despotism.

Civil Society and the Gender Division of Labor

In civil society we confront a very specific idea of the individual. It is the auto-determined individual, in whom any determination that has not been generated by his own choice is represented as external to him, and, so far as it constrains him, as an obstacle or impediment to his freedom. The assertion of individuality is, simultaneously, the assertion of the individual's freedom from all objects and persons outside himself, an assertion of his separateness.

The theory of civil society accounts for this individual's entering a moral relation of mutual recognition between individuals. This is done to secure the individual's existence and interest, for without a "social contract" between individuals, one would confront the perpetual uncertainties of a war of all against all. This war would arise from the way in which self-assertion leads each individual to assume his priority in relation to others. They are the means to his ends; he is not the means to theirs. What the social contract effects is a mutuality of recognition and of use, wherein each agrees to recognize the other if, in turn, he is recognized, and to serve as a means to the other's ends if, in turn, the other is prepared to serve as a means to his ends.

Certainly the social contract qualifies the rugged splendor of isolated individuality. It indicates that, in some elementary fashion, the existence of individuals is contingent on the recognition by others of their individuality. Yet this qualification does not go very far. There is nothing specific about this dependence on others. It is a universal dependency which targets neither specific others to give recognition, nor specific qualities of the individual's personality to be given recognition. Within such an abstract and formal ethos of mutual recognition, the individual can experience himself as free of any particular dependencies and, in this regard, as independent.[4] Within civil society,

---

4. As Rousseau put it, " 'The problem is to find a form of association which will defend and protect with the whole common force the person and goods of each associate, and in which each, while uniting himself with all,

then, the individual's dependency on others is expressed as an abstract and generalized fraternity, internally differentiated by competition.[5]

The counterpart of this independence of particular dependencies is mutual indifference on the part of individuals to the specific content the individuality of others assumes. There is no concern for how mutual exchange may serve the specific needs of specific individuals. From the standpoint of civil society, what is of concern is only the universality of the mutuality of use, and the translation of this universality into a universal medium of exchange.

For each individual, what remains paramount and of priority is his own interest, and the interests of others concern him only as they forward his own. Even the individual himself seeks to be free of the specific content his will assumes at any particular time by accumulating as much as possible of the universal medium of desire. In this way, his own interest assumes an abstract quality. The freedom of this individuality is bought at the price of its abstraction from any specific content. It is this which makes it the freedom, in principle at least, of infinite desire, or need.[6]

---

may still obey himself alone, and remain as free as before'. This is the fundamental problem of which the social contract provides the solution." How? Because "each man, in giving himself to all, gives himself to nobody; and as there is no associate over which he does not acquire the same right as he yields others over himself, he gains an equivalent for everything he loses, and an increase of force for the preservation of what he has."—From "The Social Contract," in J.J. Rousseau, *The Social Contract and Discourses*, ed. by G.D.H. Cole, and revised and augmented by J.H. Brumfitt and John C. Hall (London: J.M. Dent, 1973), p. 174.

5. I agree with Carole Pateman that the social contract is a fraternal contract: see her "The Fraternal Social Contract: Some Observations on Patriarchal Civil Society," forthcoming special issue of *Telos*, ed. by J. Keane.

6. Since "the object of man's desire, is not to enjoy once only, and for one instant of time; but to assure for ever, the way of his future desire, I put for a generall inclination of all mankind, a perpetuall and restlesse desire of Power after Power, that ceaseth only in Death."—Hobbes, *Leviathan*, ed. by C.B. Macpherson (Penguin Books, 1968), pp. 160–161. In the above analysis, I am also indebted to Marx's analysis of the exchange relationship, and of the

One basic problem with this construction of the individual in society has received considerable commentary in the liberal tradition. This is the problem of voluntarism. If the moral order of mutual recognition between auto-determined individuals is, perforcedly, abstract, it is liable also to disruption by the decision of any one of those individuals that they do not want to play this game any more. They may discern more immediate advantage in resorting to force or fraud against their competitors than in continuing to play by the rules. Nothing has ensured their obligation to abide by the rule of mutual recognition. Based as it is on the unconstrained choice of individuals, civil order is not particularly secure.

A further problem with this construction of the individual in society has been "seen" before, but only now begins to be "conceptualized" by feminist critics of the liberal tradition.[7] In the bracketing out of any specific dependencies of the individual and of the specific content of his individuality, the family is inevitably bracketed out of the civil conception of society. The family is consigned to the "private life" of these individuals, whereas "society" concerns their publicly manifest, abstract and nonspecifically disclosive individuality.

The logic of this is to suggest that whatever specific dependencies the family may involve, they are structured or determined by the wills of these auto-determined individuals. Otherwise they would not be auto-determined. In effect, the family is conceived as the private property of these individuals. In this respect, the family takes on the status of an object, placed within the domain of objects controlled and mastered by subject wills—the domain of "nature."

The exclusion of the family from "society" is expressed in its placement outside the morality of mutual recognition of persons. At least, this is true of relations between family members. As a unit, within civil society, the family is accorded recognition by other individuals as the private property of one among their number. Two important issues

---

translation of what Hobbes called "power" into money, in *Capital*, volume one, Part I, and in the *Grundrisse*.

7. See, e.g., Carole Pateman "Feminist Critiques of the Public-Private Dichotomy," chapter in S. Benn and G. Gauss (eds.), *Conceptions of the Public and Private in Social Life* (Croom Helm, forthcoming).

arise here. First, what are the consequences of placing the relations between human beings within the family outside the morality of civil society, especially for these civil individuals required to be masters and owners of their respective families? Second, why does the auto-determined individual of civil society need this specific set of dependencies at all?

The problem of voluntarism indicates the impossibility of the idea of civil society's generating a systematic theory of social life. The conception of social order which this idea generates breaks asunder into an opposition between the auto-determined individual and his socially located existence. The civil conception of society, which reconciles auto-determined individuality with its dependence on social recognition by means of the social contract, turns into its opposite. Society now becomes all those aspects of the social location of the individual which are not the outcome of his choice. This conception of society accommodates custom, the state and the family, all of which are counterposed to the autonomous individual.

The problem of voluntarism, then, implies the second problem of the exclusion of the family from civil society. Stripped of all specific and substantive content, the individual of civil society stands forth as, simply, will. At any particular point of time this will must take the form of a definite content. This content can be provided to the will only from without, in its particularistic features by the family, and in its universalistic features by the state. Necessarily, the family and the state are experienced as coercive forces or constraints on the individual will. Each stands for society in contradistinction to the individual will, which is why in liberal theory and public policy, the family and the state often substitute for one another.

If the idea of civil society precludes any coherent account of civil society, the state and the family as all aspects of the same totality, it is the specific antinomy of the family and civil society on which I wish to focus. What is at issue is how the idea of civil society invokes the idea of the individual will, the specific content of whose individuality must be bestowed and recognized by another who is outside civil relations but within the individual's family, and whose connection to the individual will must be suppressed if that will is to remain free.

Specific individuality has two aspects. First, the existence of an individual as a will requires a form of recognition which the mutuality of civil society precludes. The primacy of the individual will is qualified in civil society. To assert itself, it requires another which accords it primacy by denying itself to be a separate and autonomous will.

Second, the specific content the willing of an individual assumes requires a recognition which the universality of reciprocal use and recognition of civil society cannot provide. This content may change, but at any particular moment its specific and concrete quality must be affirmed. Again, it is only another *outside* civil society (who does not, therefore, translate the specific content of the individual's will into a universal denominator) who can provide this affirmation. This other does so by adopting the specific content of the individual's will as the governing purpose or end of its own action. By doing so, this other is delegated responsibility for the specific content of the individual's will (his desires), thereby keeping the latter free to assume that his civil pursuit of infinite desire is more real than what he sees as the merely contingent quality of his desires at any particular time.

Again, the individuals of civil society require another order of persons, lying outside civil society and within the family, whose *raison d'être* is to affirm the existence of the former as wills. Love is the form this affirmation takes. Civil society, then, rests on a relationship of domination between subject wills and others, a relationship which is articulated outside civil society and within the family, such that the appearance of civil society as the domain of reciprocal freedom and equality can be sustained.

It is a division of labor between subject wills and others. The instrumental orientation of the former in actualizing the universality of mutual recognition and use is sustained by the expressive orientation of the latter, in upholding the integrity of those subject wills as primary and specific wills.

For this division of labor to appear normative, there must be a division of humanity which provides these two categories of persons. Sex difference is this division in that culture associates one sex with the freedom of willing, and the other only with the capacity to follow the former's willing. This is because natural determination is conceived to qualify the latter's freedom to will.

The individuals of civil society are masculine individuals, and the others, on whom they depend for specific recognition, are feminine individuals. Civil society and the sexual division of labor are reciprocally dependent.

Since the individuals of civil society are masculine, their freedom is already seriously qualified in being subject to this masculine determination. In order to assert their freedom *within* civil society, these individuals must bracket out the relevance and significance of their shared masculinity, and thus affirm the abstract universality of civil society. To bracket out their determination as masculine individuals within civil society, they must deny the dependency of themselves, and of civil society in general, on women, and on the family, respectively.[8] Thus it is that their autonomy as separate wills within civil society takes the form of independence and separateness from specific dependencies. At the same time, the bracketing out of the masculine determination of civil individuality means that formal access to civil society for women cannot be precluded.

It is not simply, then, that these masculine wills require a set of others, women, who, in order to accord specific recognition to the former, must abdicate their own wills, and subject themselves within personal relations to men. Beyond this, these masculine wills deny the necessity of this relation of domination, and deny the reality of these feminine others on whom they depend. For this denial to work, the subjectivity of these feminine others must be denied an autonomous existence, as it is in the conception of them as lying within the private property of individual masculine wills. Hence the masculine will is not dependent on another subject: his freedom is not qualified thereby. On the contrary, his freedom is affirmed by his being shown to be the master of a specific category of objects which have the most

---

8. This denial has been explored at the level of ontogenetic analysis by feminist critical reworking of the "oedipal crisis." See, in particular, Nancy Chodorow, *The Reproduction of Mothering: Psychoanalysis and the Sociology of Gender* (Berkeley: University of California Press, 1978); and Jessica Benjamin *op.cit.* However, it is hoped this paper begins to make a contribution to analysis of this denial at the level of the idea society has of itself, a level hitherto neglected.

remarkable and valuable qualities of being able to accord the master personal recognition and service.

Because the masculine individual–master denies the status of autonomous subject to these others on whom he depends, his will in regard to them is unconstrained by any requirement of mutual recognition between subjects. Accordingly, within the family, he asserts his will in a form which expresses this lack of constraint. This form is whim, or caprice.

The essential problem with this set-up resides in the denial of autonomous subjectivity to those whose special role it is to confirm the specific individuality of masculine wills. The problem does not lie with the need for the feminine other to recognize or to service the content the masculine will assumes as this or that desire at any particular time. The problem lies in ensuring that this desire is accorded recognition as an expression of the freedom of willing. For this desire to be more than a determinate, given need, and to testify to the freedom of the individual who has this desire, it is his will rather than the desire in itself which must be accorded recognition. However, another whose existence belongs to his will as part of his private property cannot provide this recognition. As his property, she may be consumed, and fulfil his desire: to this extent, the act of her consumption confirms the willing agency of the masculine subject. Yet, his consumption of her as an object of his desire leaves him entirely alone, and bereft of any subject who can recognize and affirm his freedom in such mastery of the object world. It is at this point the masculine subject turns to his peers, his brother, masculine wills. But, he can solicit their recognition only in civil society, and there is no way the abstract quality of this recognition will suffice to recognize and confirm the specific act of mastery he has achieved within his family.

The problem does not end there. If the autonomous subjectivity of feminine others is denied, it reasserts itself in the way in which the abdication of their wills is in appearance only. The feminine other obeys the masculine will and, in so doing, adopts his will in place of her own. This is true as far as the objectification—the translation into being-for-others—of the will goes, but what of the pre-objectified will, the will as unstated intention? Since the relation between masculine will and feminine other takes the form of a subject–object relation, their relation is entirely external. This is expressed in the way in which her will automatically follows his, as an object follows its owner. The externality of their relation precludes the masculine will from understanding or knowing what is in the mind of his feminine other.

Since his will or mind is hers, she does not have a will or mind of her own for him to understand. The result of this is that her thoughts and intentions, so far as they are not expressed to him, become placed completely outside his knowledge or awareness. If, then, she plans to revolt against his rule of her, when this revolt occurs it comes as a complete surprise to him. Or, she may outwardly conform to his will, when, all the time, inwardly, and perhaps as expressed to her fellow, feminine others, she may feel complete lack of respect for his will. This is not unlikely, since the externality of their relation constrains him to assert himself through whim and caprice. The masculine will's mastery of the feminine other reveals itself to be based in the willingness of that other to deceive him that he is both master and free. At the same time, the confinement of the feminine other to pre-objectivated willing means her confinement to the irreality and irresponsibility of pure intentions.

That civil society should require domestic despotism, and that together they constitute a relational whole are not ideas which liberal commentary on the idea of civil society has chosen to note. Tied in with this has been the failure on the part of liberal commentary to bring out the way in which the individuals of civil society are inherently despotic. This failure is odd, since all the classical theorists of civil society represent its outcome as despotism. Hobbes actually legitimizes this outcome in the *Leviathan,* while Locke and Rousseau attempt to secure a non-despotic civil government but see it as inevitably degenerating into despotism.

Despotism is the necessary tendency of the auto-determined will which, in asserting its freedom, seeks to claim priority in regard to all other wills. Despotism is the effective establishment by force or fraud of one individual's priority in regard to the rest in civil society: it is his will which subdues and commands their wills. For Locke and Rousseau there is, ultimately, effective revolt against tyranny, and the social contract, or moral order of mutual recognition of wills, is re-established. Effectively, there is a perpetual cycle of an orderly civil society, disruption of that order and ensuing despotism, followed by re-establishment of civil society.

The point must be that despotism is a necessary tendency of the auto-determined will and is, thus, an inherent moment within civil society. It is unlikely to congeal into an institutionalized tyranny precisely because of the condition of competition between all individual wills, and their refusal to subject themselves to another will, except as compelled to do so through force or fraud. Such compulsion is unlikely to be efficacious for very long or on a universal scale. Thus, despotism and the rule of mutual recognition are continually operant moments within civil society with the tendency of the former to systemic disruption being checked by the systemic quality of universal competition. Despotism and democracy become, then, mutually required terms of the relation of civil society.

Montesquieu is a classical exponent of the idea of civil society who argues the necessity for civil order to be established in such a way that the tendency to despotism is effectively checked. He makes an extensive analysis of despotism, which he arraigns as a distinct societal type, "Asiatic despotism."[9]

However, "despotism" in Montesquieu's thought is more and less than a distinct societal type: it is the limiting case of all civil and political government, since it represents the breakdown of any restraints on the natural, unlimited and self-interested passions (desires) of the individual.[10] The republican type of government requires a "self-renunciation," precisely because its principle, virtue, "requires a constant preference of public to private interest."[11] While this is the most estimable type of government, Montesquieu clearly considers that, especially when the conditions of wealth are developed, the monarchical

---

9. Montesquieu's term: see "Selections from Consideration on the Causes of the Roman's Greatness and Decline," in Melvin Richter *The Political Theory of Montesquieu* (London: Cambridge University Press, 1977), p. 161.

10. This analysis is elaborated and argued in the author's "The Classical Theory of Civil Society," chapter 6.

11. Montesquieu, *The Spirit of the Laws*, translated by Thomas Nugent, and with an Introduction by Franz Neumann (N.Y.: Hafner Press, 1949) Book 4, p. 34.

type is one more suited to the reconciliation of this self of unlimited passions with political and civil order. For in this type, the individual will is afforded expression but in such a way that competition for honor effectively checks its tendency to assert itself despotically. Despotism, on the other hand, "is what every capacity may reach," and since the effective regulation of individual ambition "is a masterpiece of legislation, rarely produced by hazard and seldom attained by prudence," and, accordingly, "most nations are subject to this very government."[12]

Montesquieu, however, goes considerably farther than the other classical exponents of the idea of civil society in his proposition that there is a necessary connection between despotism in the civil domain and domestic despotism.[13] Indeed, in the *Persian Letters,* Montesquieu offers an extended and brilliant analysis of the structure of domestic despotism.

Arguably, Montesquieu reserves this connection between civil and domestic despotism to cases where despotism has become institutionalized as the type of government. Yet, if despotism is granted to be an inherent tendency in civil society, the implications of this connection go much farther. It is also to be remarked that while the *Persian Letters* situate domestic despotism within the societal type of Asiatic despotism, the domestic despot of these letters is a Persian courtier who is enlightened and educated, and who leaves the court as a protest against its corruption. His domestic tyranny, then, is to be arraigned against his civilized or civil character,[14] and, accordingly, allows us to

---

12. Montesquieu, *The Spirit of the Laws,* Book 5, p. 62.

13. ". . . the slavery of women is perfectly conformable to the genius of a despotic government, which delights in treating all with severity. Thus at all times have we seen in Asia domestic slavery and despotic government walk hand in hand with an equal pace."—Montesquieu, *The Spirit of the Laws,* Book 15, p. 256.

14. Mary Lyndon Shanley and Peter S. Stillman make a similar point in their "Political and Marital Despotism: Montesquieu's Persian Letters," in Jean Bethke Elshtain ed. *The Family in Political Thought* (Armherst: University of Massachusetts Press), p. 78: "Precisely because Usbek is in many respects a congenial, intelligent, and even admirable man, Montesquieu's con-

explore the connection between civil society and domestic despotism.

Before I turn to Montesquieu's analysis of domestic despotism in the case of this Persian courtier's seraglio, it is important to emphasize that the brilliance and import of this analysis has been virtually ignored in commentary on his work.[15] This is the case even when we take into account the way in which recent feminist standards of cultural relevance have generated serious analyses of Montesquieu's use of the seraglio in the *Persian Letters*.[16] Such neglect of the general significance of Montesquieu's analysis of domestic despotism for his and our idea of civil society is testimony to the degree to which modern political and social theory is structured by the masculine denial of the mutual dependence of civil society and domestic despotism.

---

demnation of the corruption that domestic tyranny works on otherwise good men is all the more compelling. Usbek is clearly a man of enlightenment." However, Shanley and Stillman focus on these corrupting effects of despotism, in both its public and domestic expressions, and they do not note nor investigate the kind of individuality—civil individuality—that Montesquieu makes the condition of despotism, both domestic and public.

15. A possible exception to this is Marshall Berman's stress on the significance of the *Persian Letters* in his *The Politics of Authenticity: Radical Individualism and the Emergence of Modern Society* (London: Allen and Unwin, 1971). It is no accident that Berman wrote this book under the immediate stimuli of the "New Left," and of the newly emerged "Women's Liberation Movement," whose slogan "the personal is the political" clearly powerfully influenced him. (see his "Introduction: The Personal is Political," especially pp. xv–xvi). However in defining the type of individuality that requires expression in domestic despotism as "inauthentic," Berman evades analysis of this type of individuality and of its existence and implications as the general model for what it is to be a modern individual.

16. In addition to the works by Stanley and Stillman, and by Berman, cited above, see also: Robert F. O'Reilly, "Montesquieu: Anti-feminist," *Studies on Voltaire and the Eighteenth-Century*, 102 (1973): 143–157; and Sheila Mason, "The Riddle of Roxane," in Eve Jacobs et al. (eds.), *Woman and Society in Eighteenth-Century France* (London: the Athlone Press, 1979).

Domestic Despotism in Montesquieu's Persian Letters

The *Persian Letters* are a series of letters to and from two Persians, Usbek and Rica, who are travelling from Persia to the West, where they spend the principal part of their journey in France. Usbek is the leader of the expedition, with Rica his junior partner. Usbek appears to be the only one of the two to be married, and it is his seraglio which occupies a central place in the letters to and from him.

While there is an element of narrative structure in the letters generated by the length of time Usbek and Rica are abroad and by the deepening of their acquaintance with the West, this structure only becomes a developed narrative in relation to the impact of Usbek's absence on the seraglio, and to the events which unfold in it. The letter opening the work is from Usbek to a male friend, arguably a letter between civil individuals; the second letter is from Usbek, giving instructions to the Chief Black Eunuch, left in charge of Usbek's seraglio in his absence; and the letter which closes the work (L. 161) is a letter from one of Usbek's wives, which contains a passionate and eloquent protest against his domestic despotism.

The domestic despot is both husband and master. The *Persian Letters* demonstrate that each of these roles is required to mediate the other if the structure of domestic despotism is to remain intact. So, the husband must sanction the love relation he has with his wives by mastery and, ultimately, force over them; and the master must mediate and temper his authority over his wives by love. The structure of the seraglio allows the domestic despot to delegate the immediately coercive aspect of his role as master to the male eunuchs who guard and serve the wives. Usbek's absence does not change this. What Usbek's absence does mean is the removal of the mediation of mastery by love, and the contraction of the husband–master's role to immediate mastery, and it is this which upsets the equilibrium of the seraglio and causes it to fall into progressive disorder.

Thus, three of the early letters (Letters 3, 4 and 7) can be read as protests from three of Usbek's wives against the removal of the mediation of his mastery by his love. Two of these letters (Letters 3 and 7) interpret Usbek's readiness to leave his wives as an index of their dispensability as far as he is concerned: he does not appear to need their love,

166

while their very existence is to be consumed by love for him, which, in the case of his absence, must go unfulfilled. Thus, Fatme writes (Letter 7) Usbek:

> How wretched a woman is, having such violent desires, when she is deprived of the only man who can appease them; when, left to herself, with nothing to distract her, she must habitually spend her time in longing, in a frenzy of unsatisfied desire; when, so far from being contented, she has not even got the consolation of being necessary to someone else's contentment; a useless ornament in a seraglio, kept for the honour, not the happiness, of her husband![17]

By travelling abroad, Usbek has placed himself outside the domestic domain and in the civil domain. His absence, thus, becomes understandably equated with the civil individual's denial of his specific dependencies and, by extension, of those on whom he depends.

Given this meaning of his absence, the wives displace the centrality of Usbek's recognition to the maintenance of their identity, and look to gain such recognition elsewhere. It is this process of displacement of Usbek's centrality to them which provides a narrative of progressive disorder in the seraglio.

The first signs of disorder are, in themselves, slight, but prove to be the beginnings of this process. At first, it is acts of individual wives which cause the exclusivity of their love for Usbek to be suspected.[18] However, disorder becomes more generalized in the development of quarrels between the wives, as reported by the Chief Black Eunuch in Letter 64, where he asks Usbek to give him a completely free hand in re-establishing order by whatever method necessary:

> The seraglio is in appalling disorder and confusion. Your wives are at war with one another, your eunuchs on different sides. There is nothing to be heard but complaints, protests, and recriminations. My admonitions are ignored. It seems as if nothing is forbidden in this time of laxity, and my title has no meaning in the seraglio.[19]

---

17. Montesquieu, *Persian Letters,* translated with an introduction and notes by C.J. Betts (Penguin Books, 1973), p. 47.

18. See Montesquieu, *Persian Letters,* Letters 4 (p. 44) and 20 (pp. 67–69).

19. Montesquieu, *Persian Letters,* p. 130.

Usbek responds, and appeals to his wives to abide by their promise to him when he left to live together peacefully, threatening that if they do not, he will have to give the Chief Eunuch free rein in his handling of them. His letter ends:

> I urge you, then, to change your conduct, and behave in such a way that I shall be able to reject, another time, the suggestions which have been put to me, and which are prejudicial to your freedom and peace of mind.
>
> For I would like you to forget that I am your master, and remember only that I am your husband.[20]

A considerable break in any further reports of trouble in the seraglio gives the impression that things settle down for a while. However, the tension continues to mount and erupts in acts of infidelity and a complete breakdown of authority in the seraglio (Letter 147). Now Usbek gives the Chief Eunuch "unlimited powers over the entire seraglio,"[21] but the Chief Eunuch, clearly a man to be feared, dies before he can execute his newly gained power. His authority devolves on an old and ineffectual eunuch, whose habit of uncritical obedience prevents him from opening Usbek's letter giving the Chief Eunuch a free rein (Letters 149 and 151). The Chief Eunuch foresaw the probable failure of his successor, and has prepared another eunuch, keen and tough in his role as a guard of the wives' virtue, to warn Usbek of what may develop.

It is this eunuch, Solim, who reports (Letter 151) the abandonment of all restraint on the part of the wives, with the exception of Usbek's beloved Roxana: "Only Roxana has remained dutiful and continues

---

20. Montesquieu, *Persian Letters*, L. 65, p. 133.

21. "Let fear and terror be your companions; go with all speed to punish and chastise in room after room; everyone must live in dread, everyone must weep before you. Interrogate the whole seraglio, beginning with the slaves. Do not spare the women whom I love; each of them must undergo this terrible investigation. Expose the darkest secrets, purify this place of infamy, and bring back virtue from its exile."—Montesquieu, *Persian Letters*, L. 148, p. 271.

to behave with decorum."[22] This accords with Usbek's earlier (Letter 26) imputation to Roxana of a "natural," as distinct from an enforced virtue, because he interprets her resistance to his "possession" of her when they first married as a "struggle between love and virtue."[23] Roxana herself sustains this belief in her by a letter to Usbek which records and protests the terrible punishments visited on the wives by Solim, who now has been entrusted by Usbek with authority over them. The tone of this letter suggests the wrongful punishment of one who is virtuous; at the same time, its anger is real, and contains rebellion:

> A squad of new eunuchs has been brought into the seraglio, and they besiege us night and day; our sleep is constantly being interrupted by their suspicions, real or imaginary. My consolation is that all this will not last for long, and that these miseries will end with my life. It will not be a long one, cruel Usbek; I shall not give you the time to put a stop to all these outrages.[24]

The third to last letter in the *Persian Letters* is from Solim to Usbek, reporting Roxana's infidelity, the shock of which is a function of her hitherto unquestioned virtue:

> Roxana, the proud Roxana, oh gods! who is to be trusted henceforward? You suspected Zelis, and were entirely sure of Roxana. But her stern virtue was a cruel trick, a veil which covered treachery. I caught her in the arms of a young man . . . . The eunuchs came running . . . and surrounded him; he defended himself for a long time . . . . He even wanted to get back into the bedroom, so as to die, he said, before Roxana's eyes. But finally he yielded to numbers and fell at our feet.[25]

The very last letter, (Letter 161) is from Roxana herself, written as she is dying by her own hand. This letter makes it clear that she has

---

22. Montesquieu, *Persian Letters*, p. 273.

23. Montesquieu, *Persian Letters*, p. 76.

24. Montesquieu, *Persian Letters*, L. 156, p. 277.

25. Montesquieu, *Persian Letters*, L. 159, p. 279.

always hated Usbek,[26] and that this infidelity occurred through a genuine and long-harbored love for the young man:

> You should even be grateful to me for the sacrifice that I made on your account, for having demeaned myself so far as to seem faithful to you, for having had the cowardice to guard in my heart something that I ought to have revealed to the whole earth, and finally for having profaned the name of virtue by permitting it to be applied to my acceptance of your whims.[27]

Usbek's wives are clearly his private property: some of them have been bought as slaves, and the free-born among them are represented as enslaved by their love for him.[28] This enslavement is literal. Usbek's wives are required to love him, at least as far as all outward appearance can suggest, and their orientation to him as a love-object is enforced by sanctions preventing its transfer elsewhere. The wives are veiled in public—i.e. outside the privacy of their own rooms—and these veiled faces represent both the appearance of unqualified love for their husband and their lack of access to men other than their husband. In effect, the veil marks the wives as the private property of their husband.

Usbek must believe that his wives love him as a husband rather than obey him as a master, because, unless there is a voluntary element in their submission to him, his will cannot be given recognition by theirs.[29] At the same time he cannot really credit the existence of this voluntary element because he *possesses*—in both senses of the word—his wives' love. Accordingly, up until the point when he is informed of her treachery, he is completely sure of Roxana's love for

---

26. "You were surprised not to find one carried away by the ecstasy of love; if you had known me properly you would have found in me all the violence of hate."—Montesquieu, *Persian Letters,* p. 281.

27. Montesquieu, *Persian Letters,* L. 161, p. 281.

28. Fatme writes Usbek, "What can you expect a woman to do when she loves you; . . . a free woman, by the accident of birth, but enslaved by the violence of her love?"—Montesquieu, *Persian Letters,* L. 7, p. 46.

29. See Jessica Benjamin, "The Bonds of Love: Rational Violence and Erotic Domination."

him. However, the relation of possession means Usbek cannot derive recognition as a husband, as a loved individual from his wives: he can gain recognition only as a master, and through the outward show of love, since fear is the bottom line of his wives' submission to him.[30] The voluntary element does not enter into whether his wives appear to love him: it enters into whether the appearance of their love is real or not. The critical point is that it is only the wives, and never Usbek, who can know this, as Roxana's last letter makes clear:

> How could you have thought me credulous enough to imagine that I was in the world only to worship your caprices? that while you allowed yourself everything, you had the right to thwart all my desires? No: I may have lived in servitude, but I have always been free. I have amended your laws according to the laws of nature, and my mind has always remained independent.[31]

Hence it becomes clear that, if the veil marks the wives as the private property of the master–husband, it can also be used by the wives as defensive cover, and can rebound against the husband–master.

All Usbek confronts is a mirror in the outward show of love of his wives for him. He can obtain only negative recognition of his will in his acknowledgment of the inner life of his wives in his constant suspicion and jealousy with regard to them: "I seem not to exist any more, and I become aware of myself again only when lurking jealousy flares up in my heart and there breeds alarm, suspicion, hatred and regret."[32]

The character of this recognition requires Usbek to suppress the wills of his wives, the ultimate expression of which is to order their

---

30. Rica writes to Usbek: "With us everyone's character is uniformly the same, because they are forced. People do not seem what they are, but what they are obliged to be. Because of this enslavement of heart and mind, nothing is heard but the voice of fear, which has only one language, instead of nature, which expresses itself so diversely and appears in so many different forms."—Montesquieu, *Persian Letters*, L. 63, pp. 129–130.

31. Montesquieu, *Persian Letters*, L. 161, p. 280.

32. Montesquieu, *Persian Letters*, L. 155, p. 275.

deaths. At this point, he does not even confront a mirror: he is left alone and uncertain of his existence.

As to the wives, the voluntary element in their submission is of a kind as to keep their wills pre-objectivated and at the level only of intentions. Roxana must die once her will takes on objectivated expression and becomes unveiled, since she is not allowed to have a will of her own.

This state of affairs is like the "state of nature," i.e. the state in which the individual will is placed when there is no social contract. The difference resides in its being only Usbek's will which claims priority in relation to those of his wives, with the attendant necessity that he dominate them. The wives' wills are asserted not in a public, competitive struggle for priority in relation to Usbek's will, but in an internal struggle to keep their wills "veiled" and detached from their outwardly manifest behavior. The necessity of their wills to remain un-actualized in social terms is the other side of the primacy of Usbek's will taking expression in the publicly manifest ownership of his wives and their wills.

Usbek has set up this situation in which he can never knowingly attain the freely given love of his wives. He needs to be loved, but he has to express this need in a form which attests to his freedom from specific dependencies. This contradiction in terms is expressed in the way in which his need for love must take the form of ownership of his love-objects and thereby ensure the lack of fulfilment of that need.

In this case, the logical extension of love as ownership is made. Not only does Usbek literally own his wives, with complete freedom of use in regard to them, including the right to destroy them, but his freedom from specific dependencies is expressed in his possessing not one wife but many. Usbek ensures his freedom through generalizing his need to be loved at the cost of losing any real knowledge of those whose role it is to love him:

> It is not, Nessir [a Persian friend of Usbek's to whom he is writing], that I love them. In the crowded seraglio in which I live, I forestalled and destroyed love by love itself; but from my very lack of feeling has come a secret jealousy which is devouring me. I see a troup of women virtually left to themselves; I have only men of debased souls to answer for them.

I could scarcely feel secure if my slaves were faithful. What will it be like if they are not?[33]

Usbek goes on to bring out the way in which the civil rule of mutual recognition between masculine individuals cannot extend to providing him with support as far as his domestic life goes, because it is confined to being his private property. All that may be civilly recognized is whether he effectively owns this property or not, and if, somehow, he has lost control over it, that can only diminish the extent of recognition he gains as a private property owner from others. Thus Usbek continues his lament to his friend, Nessir:

> It is an evil for which my friends can provide no remedy: the seraglio is a place whose unhappy secrets they must ignore. For what could they do there? Would not impunity and concealment be a thousand times preferable to public chastisement. I commit all my woes to your heart, my dear Nessir; it is the only consolation left to me in the present state.

If love turns out to be chimerical in the seraglio, mastery must be real. Usbek's freedom of specific dependencies must be expressed also in his freedom from the immediacy and specific character of mastery of specific others. This task is delegated to the eunuchs. Their role cannot be assumed by other women, because women cannot share in the authority of the socially objectivated will. It is men who must fulfil this role, then, but if they are not to vie with the husband–master in his possession of the wives, they must be deprived of their ability to master them through love, and they must be themselves possessions, i.e. slaves, of the master.

The eunuchs are compensated for their loss of a husband's sexual power through their acquisition of immediate power over the women. Indeed, the eunuchs do not require to love, or be loved by, the women since they do not participate in the individuality of civil society. As slaves, they are like "things," and can be placed in relation to others only as things which do or do not externally constrain them. If Usbek's need to own the particular category of things that the wives

---

33. Montesquieu, *Persian Letters*, L. 6, p. 46.

represent requires him to conceive his ownership as love rather than mastery, the eunuchs can conceive their power over the women as free of such a compromising element. Thus, the Chief Eunuch writes:

> When my first master formed the cruel plan of entrusting his wives to me, and had compelled me, by inducements backed up by immediate threats, to be separated from myself for ever, I thought . . . that I should be sacrificing my desires for the sake of my peace of mind and my career. Unhappy wretch that I was, with my preconceived ideas I could see only the advantages, not the deprivations. I anticipated that I should be freed from the onset of love by my powerlessness to satisfy it. But alas! the effects of my passions were eliminated, but not their cause; and far from finding relief, I found myself surrounded by scenes which continually aroused them . . . .
>
> Finally, the fires of youth are past . . . I can look at women without emotion, and am paying them back for all their contempt, and all the torments that they have made me suffer. I never forget that I was born to command over them, and it is as if I become a man again on the occasions when I now give them orders . . . Although I keep them for another man, the pleasure of making myself obeyed gives me a secret joy. When I deny them everything, if it as if I was doing it on my own behalf. . . . The seraglio for me is like a little empire, and my desire for power, the only emotion which remains to me, is to some extent satisfied.[34]

As I have argued, the masculine individual will does not, and cannot, admit the way in which his specific dependency on others in his domestic life constrains him to express this dependency as his mastery and domination over these others. This is why the eunuchs are required to be an element in the picture: they are to represent that aspect of the master's self which he cannot directly acknowledge as part of his self. In effect, then, the separate personae of the husband–master and of the eunuchs are simply the "acting out" of a necessary "splitting" of love and mastery as components of the civil individual's psyche. On this reading, the eunuchs are to be understood as split-off aspects of the husband–master's self rather than as his possessions or

---

34. Montesquieu, *Persian Letters*, L. 9, pp. 49–51.

slaves. In this regard, their structural status is very different from that of the wives, who are true possessions and slaves of the husband–master.

Conclusion

The analysis I have offered in this paper would suggest that the limits of patriarchal citizenship are profound. To be sure, the universality of civil society, which arises out of the necessity to bracket out the masculine determination of the individual, makes it impossible for there to be formal barriers to entry on the part of women. At least this is true so far as women can demonstrate they have the social capacities to participate as willing individuals in civil society.

The formal entry of women into civil society, though, has not qualified the substantive masculine determination of the individual will except insofar as the implicit challenge it involves begins to recast civil society and civil individuality as something other than they are. Given the framework of civil society and the idea of the individual it entails, the formal entry of women into it has meant 1) the enforced acquisition of masculine individuality on the part of those few women who successfully advance their claims as subject wills, and 2) the more general translation into the public domain of the masculine will—feminine other relation and dialectic. The public domain has thereby taken on aspect of both civil society *and* domestic despotism. This is expressed most neatly in the so-called gender segmentation of the public workforce.

At the same time, in both civil and domestic domains, the dialectic of masculine will and feminine other has generated a dynamic of challenge to the masculine determination and limitation of individuality. Men's need for love—whether as husbands or sons—has required them progressively to bestow on women a substantive will of their own which, in the same measure, has required men to surrender their mastery over women.

The working out of this dialectic will inevitably develop a new idea of the individual in which freedom is not irreconcilable with the need for recognition of specific individuality, and with acknowledgment of personal dependencies. The universalization of subjective agency that this entails directly contradicts the structure of current civil society;

and it is the developed character of this contradiction which today accounts for the emergence of the nature of family relationships as a political issue.

8
CONSEQUENCES OF SEIZING THE
REINS IN THE HOUSEHOLD:
A MARXIST-FEMINIST CRITIQUE
OF MARX AND ENGELS

Lorenne M. G. Clark
Clark and Associates
Digby, Nova Scotia, Canada

The Consequences of Seizing
The Reins in the Household:
A Marxist-Feminist Critique
of Marx and Engels
Lorenne M. G. Clark

The Role of Reproduction in Marxist Theory*

The political philosophy developed by Marx and Engels marked a
sharp and decisive break with the tradition of political theory that
existed prior to it (and which continued despite it). Marxism was significantly different from the theories which preceded it because it was
as much as anything a theory about political theory. What it offers is a
description of the nature and development of political theory. Its objective is to show that all political theories are irrelevant insofar as they
are thought to be true accounts of how social life came to be organized, or insofar as they are believed to be eternally adequate moral
justification for particular forms of social organization. Further, Western political theories preceding Marxism, and most of those coming
after it, assume that social life is an outgrowth of individual life—that
forms of social organization develop because of traits and qualities
which are true of generic "man."

The first major deviation from this tradition occurred when Rousseau suggested and Hegel developed the idea that there was no

---

* In this essay "reproduction" refers to the processes of childbearing and
childrearing, and "reproductive labor" to the expenditure of labor power in
bearing and rearing children.

"fixed" human nature. Marx and Engels took this further by arguing that the fundamental determinants of both social life and individual consciousness are the material conditions in which people find themselves, i.e. the way in which they must labor to provide for their sustenance and survival. In failing to identify the material reasons for particular social forms, past theories have either inadvertently or intentionally justified the fact that some persons dominate and exploit others. In this view, political theories are simply rationalizations of the status quo. Inequalities in the distribution of material goods and non-material things which the possession of material goods makes possible arise from the fact that individuals have different abilities to gain material goods because some have control of the means of production and some do not.

Marxism's account of historical change dictates a strategy to those who are least advantaged within existing forms. It tells them how they may escape their bondage. But it must first convince people that its story is correct, and show that other theories which appear to explain and also to justify inequality are false. Within Marxist theory all political theories are "inessential" (though useful) to the status quo. They are part of an ideological superstructure which arises out of a real substructure of relations which give rise to existing forms of social organization. But they are not true descriptions of the substructure which determines the specific form of a particular social organization. What is meant in referring to theories as "ideologies" is that they (1) provide a coherent system of beliefs which (2) justify the status quo but (3) are, in fact, false. At least part of what is meant by referring to them as "superstructural" is that, while they arise from the real substructure of social relations, neither they nor the substructures they describe are part of the real substructure. Without the substructural underpinnings provided by the real relations of production, existing social forms and their purportedly explanatory and justificatory superstructures would collapse.

So far as Marxism itself is concerned, I believe it delineates a form of productive relations which is more accurate than capitalism's, but I do not exempt it from criticism. While Marx and Engels made an advance by developing the view that relations between men are *social* rather than natural, their theory is incomplete because it does not acknowledge the extent to which relations between men and women are also social and not natural. While they had a fully social view of men, they had only a partially social view of women, and of the relations between men and women. While they understood that the relations between men are a result of their productive relationship, they did not see that the relations between men and women are determined by their relationship to reproduction. And while they recognized that relations between men could be fundamentally altered by changing the relations of production, they did not recognize that the relations between men and women could be altered only by changing their relationships to reproduction.

The problems I have with Marxism relate to the issue of reproduction. The view that I am going to develop is that Marxism was correct in identifying the sources of inequality as between classes of men, but I want to argue beyond this that Marxism does not identify the cause of inequality between men and women. It does not see that differential ownership of private property as between males and females is a real cause of existing social forms and of sexual inequality. It does not consider the substructure of reproductive relations (which preserves the status quo between the *sexes*).

Today's system is not just a system of private property, but one of private property *under male control*. The fact that private property was under individual *male* ownership has necessitated sexual inequality not only in the ownership of the means and products of production, but also in those of reproduction. It was men's seizing of the "reins in the household," appropriating rights of ownership over the means and products of reproduction, that brought about sexual inequality even in the distribution of labor. Marx and Engels did not appreciate this because they did not acknowledge the significance of the fact that capitalism was a system of private property under *male* ownership, rather than a system of private property with unequal distribution only among classes. They failed to appreciate the extent to which sexual inequality was based not on a "natural" division of labor between the sexes, but on social conventions designed to ensure both continuing male ownership of private property and continuing female performance of reproductive labor. Marx and Engels failed to see that the division of labor between the sexes was a product rather than a cause of the fact that males came to control existing forms of private property.

Further, insofar as Marxist theory does not address itself to the issue of ownership and control of the means and products of reproduction, it is just as defective as other political theories, all of which refuse to acknowledge that reproduction is a public, political, and economic problem, a form of labor as necessary to the maintenance of society as productive labor, and just as much in need of public regulation and control to ensure that it is non-exploitative. Marx and Engels wished to bring women into the productive labor force, and they thought they could do so by socializing at least some of the work of child-rearing. However, they still appeared to believe that children would be born as a consequence of the "natural" association of the sexes, and that something like a traditional family and a traditional division of labor within it would persist. The major difference they saw between the family under capitalism and the family under socialism was that under socialism women would be free to enter the labor market and hence would not be in a position of economic dependence. This leaves unanswered questions about who would be doing the reproductive work whether in the home or elsewhere; about who would have control over sex and reproduction in the marital setting; about who would control the design of the institutions which would relieve women of at least some domestic tasks; and about who would make decisions about demands on productive labor which would affect women insofar as they had any "unique" relation to reproduction.

Marx and Engels did not acknowledge that the existing system of private reproductive relations was necessary to the maintenance of existing non-private productive relations. They did not acknowledge that the latter was in fact maintained by denying women rights of both reproductive, and productive control. Again, traditional political theory rationalized both inequality in the distribution of private property between classes of males *and* exclusive male control of that private property. Marx and Engels clearly saw the first rationalization, but they did not so clearly see the second. To the extent that they saw it at all, they did not see that the inequality resulting from unequal ownership of private property (between males and females) would not be overcome simply by allowing women access to ownership and control of the means of production; they did not see that women cannot be the equals of men in relation to production until men are the equals of women in relation to reproduction.

I hope to show that acceptance of this thesis does not entail throwing over Marxism's premise as to the importance of private property. Indeed, I want to argue that the emergence of private property accounts for the development of both class and sexist society. But Marxism as it now stands does not, and cannot, show that sexual inequality is a product of class inequality and is, therefore, part of capitalism's ideological superstructure. It is my contention that sexual inequality is not superstructural and that Marxism fails because it shares traditional political theory's assumptions about the differential reproductive natures of men and women. It does not provide a true description of the historical position of women or of the part played by the inequality between men and women in the historical development of capitalism; it does not address itself to the issue of ensuring egalitarian reproductive relations and it does not provide a theoretical framework for resolving conflicts between the demands of production and those of reproduction.

Reproductive Labor and the Problem of Class Identity

Marx and Engels did differ from political theorists who preceded them in that they explicitly acknowledged that women were "oppressed." While prior theorists had acknowledged that women had a different role than men, and that they were properly excluded from public, political, and economic life, none of them acknowledged this as unjust. To them, the inequality between the sexes, and any alleged inferiority of women, followed from the fact that women were significantly different from men in that they could bear (and rear) children. It was argued that this biological difference with respect to women's relation to reproduction placed them at a disadvantage and justified their social and economic subjugation. According to this view, if biology leads to a disadvantage, it is not unjust since it results from natural causes. These must be accepted as part of the way things are. Marx and Engels did recognize that the position of women was not only unequal, but that this was unjustified. They argued all inequality should,

183

with the dawning of a new age, disappear. The question feminists must ask is whether sexual equality is, in fact, guaranteed within Marxism's equality with regard to production. And, hence, whether it will occur "inevitably."

It is my position that although Marx and Engels may have wanted sexual equality, and may have sincerely believed that this would be accomplished by the overthrow of class inequality, there is no guarantee that this is so. Indeed, it is far from clear that the creation of a classless society would be identical with, or would lead to, a sexually egalitarian society.

The belief that it must rests on the conviction that the inferior status of women is due solely to the fact that women are denied access to ownership of the means of production, or, to put it somewhat differently, that women's status, like that of working-class men, is determined entirely by their relation to the forces of production. What this fails to acknowledge is that *all* women are disadvantaged relative to men as a group. It is not simply that women are disadvantaged relative to middle- and upper-class men, as are working-class men. Marx and Engels, of course, are committed to the view that the creation of a classless society would bring about sexual equality because all forms of inequality are ultimately rooted in class inequality and its material origins. But what is at issue is the question as to whether or not sexual inequality is the product of class inequality, whether or not the inferior status of women is wholly accounted for by their disadvantaged position in relation to production.

In the Marxist view the development and maintenance of class society requires that the means of production be concentrated in the hands of one group of persons, who become the dominant class. If sexual inequality is to be shown to be superstructural, a *result* of class society, then it must be shown that class society necessitates, or is at least more easily, effectively, or efficiently, maintained by the creation of sexual inequality. Given that there is a dialectical relationship between classes such that there is conflict between the dominant and the disadvantaged class, it will, of course, be in the interest of the dominant class to create an even more disadvantaged class since this will produce conflict between the new and the old disadvantaged classes, with the old attempting to consolidate its gains and to curtail the gains

184

of the new. Since each class works in its own interest, the creation of a more disadvantaged class is simply a specific instance of the tactic of divide and rule. Racial inequality can be fitted into this model, as can the position of Third-World countries in relation to the highly developed and industrialized nations of Europe and North America. The creation of an "even more" disadvantaged class also produces more profit for the dominant class.

By regarding women as a reserve labor pool Marxism is suggesting that women as a group are a potentially exploitable class, that is, that when it becomes desirable for the dominant class to create another class, one more disadvantaged than the existing one, women will be brought into relations of production which would bring them into the class structure. The point is that women engaged in traditional women's work are *not* considered in a class because they are not engaged in production. As a description of how persons are organized and determined within a structure of productive relations, Marxism required that persons who play no role in relation to production are invisible to and immune from analysis. Because women have historically been denied access to the productive labor market, and because reproductive labor has been extracted from women as unpaid labor, women and reproductive labor are, simply, invisible within Marxist analysis. Women have no class in the traditional role of wife and/or mother. They take their class from that of their fathers or husbands (males) who are directly related to the mode of production. Women who enter the labor force could have an independent class position, but it is not, of course, a position they have *qua* women but *qua* productive laborers.[1] Even if they are in the labor force, however, women's position is not determined entirely by the specific nature of their relation to the mode of production.[2] Under the system of property distribution and owner-

---

1. See Judith Hicks Stiehm, "The Unit of Political Analysis: Our Aristotelian Hangover," as an exploration of this same problem. In Sandra Harding and Merrill B. Hintikka (eds.), *Discovering Reality* (D. Reidel Publishing Company, 1983), pp. 31–43.

2. Well past the time at which Marx and Engels were writing, many women engaged in productive labor had no right to the wages they earned. In the wife-husband relation the wages of the wife were owned by the hus-

ship which constitute the real substructure of social relations, males until recently had the right to appropriate the labor of women, both their labor of production and of reproduction and also the fruits of both labors.

By suggesting that women in traditional roles have no independent class position, although they function as a reserve labor pool, it seems that Marxism does not treat women's traditional "work" as production. If women's work were considered production, individual women would have assignable class positions, and, indeed, all those doing the same kind of work would have the same class position because they would be related in an identical way to production. It would also follow that women would not be available as a reserve labor pool because they would already be engaged in production. Thus it seems undeniable that Marxism does not treat reproduction as a form of production, and, perhaps more importantly, that it does not treat reproductive labor as "labor." Such labor creates no exchange value; at most it has a use value.[3]

---

band. Thus, even when engaged in productive labor, women could not be said to have a class position, or at any rate, to have the same class position as a male doing the same work. After women won the right to their own wages, a problem still remained about assigning them a class position if wife and husband were differently determined to different classes. Must the family unit be the bearer of some aggregative class position? Is the family, in fact, the ontological locus of class position?

3. To the extent that a woman's role as wife led her to perform maintenance functions for her husband, then to that extent her labor is indirectly related to production since she is expending labor power in support of a member of the productive labor force. But this is at best a kind of "volunteerism" a free donation of labor made out of love rather than necessity, and it certainly is not a mode of production though it does contribute to the creation of surplus value. Women's labor of reproduction, the bearing and rearing of children from the time of conception to the time of independence, does not contribute even indirectly to the creation of surplus value and therefore lies outside the sphere of productive relations entirely, if we take Marx's definition of "labor" seriously, as expressed, for example, in the *Economic and Philosophic Manuscripts of 1844,* (Foreign Language Publishing House, Moscow, 1961), p. 29:

But if reproduction is not a form of production, then how can a change in the relations of production, such that ownership of the means of production moves from individual to collective ownership, bring about sexual equality? Collective ownership of the means of production is collective ownership by those engaged in relations of production. If women in traditional roles are excluded from the sphere of productive relations, how will their position change when ownership becomes collective? In order to be beneficiaries of collective ownership persons must be capable of being determined by modes of production. If reproductive labor is not labor, if reproduction is not production, what will there be for women engaged in such activity to become collective owners of? It is true that those women who are either the daughters or wives of men of the disadvantaged classes could hope to be somewhat better off after the revolution, but would this in any way touch the question of *sexual* equality? Whatever is meant by sexual equality, it is not exhausted by the idea that all women will have the same class position because the men with whom they are associated have the same class position. The problem of sexual inequality is not the problem of inequality between individual women, but of the inequality of women *as a group*. In order to argue that sexual inequality is superstructural, that it would disappear with the disappearance of class inequality, Marxism would have to hold that reproduction is a form of production and that reproductive labor is "labor."

And, of course, Marx and Engels sometimes talk in this way. Indeed, whenever the issue comes up specifically, reproduction is referred to as a form of production which leads indirectly to the creation of surplus value. It is also regarded as indirectly remunerated through the money paid fathers or husbands. But this simply will not do. If reproduction is a form of production, reproductive laborers should have a class position independent of that of their fathers or husbands and should be remunerated in their own right. Other forms of labor which do not directly create surplus value do entail both determinate class positions and rights of ownership over the remuneration with which

---

In political economy *labour* occurs only in the form of *wage-earning activity*. . . .

such labor is rewarded; e.g., the labor of bureaucrats or social workers.

It seems that Marxism falls back on holding women to be a reserve labor pool as a second way of explaining how women engaged in reproductive labor are related to the mode of production. This conceptualization serves to explain women's inequality as superstructural, but ultimately it, too, defines women engaged in reproductive labor as not engaged in productive labor. It may well be true that the dominant class has an interest in keeping an able-bodied portion of the population out of production in order to be able to exploit it and others more profitably at some future time. It may also be true that this provides some role for women as a group within the sphere of productive relations in that their very existence could be said to function as a curb on the demands of the least advantaged class. But this is to assign reproductive laborers only a very marginal role in the productive sphere, and still denies that the labor they now do is a form of production. Either reproduction is a form of production which entails independent class membership and entitlement to share in the collective ownership of the means of production, or reproduction is *not* a form of production, and women engaged in reproductive labor can at best be regarded as a potentially exploitable class which is not a real class but a group outside the sphere of productive relations, invisible and unanalyzable. In failing to provide an adequate analysis of the role of reproductive labor, Marx and Engels are guilty of the same error with which they charge traditional political economy, *pace* Smith and Ricardo:

> Political economy, therefore, does not recognize the unoccupied workers, the workman, in so far as he happens to be outside this labour-relationship. The cheat-thief, swindler, beggar, and unemployed man [sic]; the starving, wretched, and criminal working man—these are *figures* who do not exist for political *economy* but only for other eyes . . . . such figures are spectres outside the domain of political economy.[4]

---

4. *Ibid.*, p. 85.

So, too, are women and reproductive labor spectres outside the domain of political economy, since they, too, are outside the defined labor relationship.

While this latter, problem-laden view seems to be the one with which Marxism is stuck, it does seem to me to be the position which is closest to the truth about the historical position of women. As I stated earlier, Marx and Engels are to be commended for the fact that they at least recognized that the historical position of women was unjustified. They believed women's oppression lay in the fact that they were not free to enter the sphere of productive relations—that it was women's lack of economic independence which led to their inferior social status. Thus they argued that the road to women's emancipation lay in increasing women's access to the productive labor force. There is no feminist who can disagree with that. Whatever else it means, sexual equality does entail equal ability to gain access to the realm of productive labor.

However, Marxism seems to have shared a further view with the political theories which preceded it. Even though Marx and Engels recognized that relations between the sexes are to some extent social rather than natural,[5] they nonetheless assumed that they are natural at least to the extent that even the exploitative nature of women's position was partially rooted in a "natural" division of labor within the family. What Marxism seems to assume is that women could not enter the sphere of productive relations as completely as men because of the responsibilities their biology bestowed upon them. Thus, while Marx and Engels do not identify the sole cause of women's social position as a biological one, and do not use this to justify women's inferior position, they do use woman's capacities with respect to reproduction to explain how it was that she did not come to be in control of the surplus arising from production. They assume that males control the

---

5. For an excellent discussion of the importance of this concept, and of its centrality to feminist analysis of history, see Joan Kelly-Gadol, "The Social Relation of the Sexes: Methodological Implications of Women's History," *Signs*, Summer 1976, Vol. 1, No. 4, pp. 809–823, though I think she is somewhat over-generous in crediting Engels with a full-blown commitment to this thesis.

means of production because women are necessarily engaged in reproductive labor.

In *Capital*, Marx and Engels indicate that sex, like age, is a factor which brings about a "natural" division of labor:

> The distribution of work within the family . . . depend[s] as well upon differences of age and sex as upon natural conditions varying with the season.[6]

> Within a family . . . there springs up naturally a division of labour, caused by differences of sex and age, *a division that is consequently based on a purely physiological foundation* . . . [emphasis mine][7]

That there is a natural division of labor in the family is also attested to in the *German Ideology:*

> The division of labour is at this tribal stage still very elementary and is confined to a further extension of the natural division of labour existing in the family.[8]

> With the division of labour, in which all these contradictions are implicit, and which in its turn is based on the natural division of labour in the family . . .[9]

But we are never told how or why sex makes a difference or what else it might be that leads to this "natural" division of labor within the family. Furthermore, in a most unMarxist and undialectical fashion, we learn from *Capital* that this division of labor within the family develops *spontaneously.* Unlike other forms of the division of labor it apparently is totally unrelated to the material substructure of relations, productive or otherwise, and is as characteristic of the precapitalist family as of the capitalist family.[10] This indicates that the concept of a

---

6. *Capital,* Vol. 1, Part 1, Ch. 1, Section 4.
7. *Ibid.,* Part IV, Ch. XIV, Section 4.
8. *German Ideology,* A.
9. *Ibid.,* A.1.
10. *Capital,* I.I.I.IV, *op. cit.,* p. 89.

fundamental division of labor within the family is an undefended "given" of Marx's thought.

What is never acknowledged is the extent to which reproductive labor is simply *extracted* from women, though Engels was, I believe, closer to the truth about this matter than was Marx. Engels understood that following the emergence of private property, the function of marriage was to ensure certainty of paternity, and that certainty of paternity was itself necessary in order to ensure genuine heirs for the purpose of inheritance.[11] But this enslavement of women to individual men was necessary not only in order to provide a mechanism for property transfers across generations. It was necessary also in order to ensure *continued male ownership of* that private property, and continued performance of reproductive labor by women. Engels explicitly recognized that the position of women following the emergence of private property was a form of oppression. But what he did not say was that the *specific* form of oppression which this created for women was that they themselves were converted into a form of private property which was available for the ownership of males. While he came closest to saying this in the *Origin of the Family, Private Property, and the State,* and indeed ought to have said it, given the analysis he gave of the relation and development of the family and private property, he did not say it. Even though in the *Origin* and elsewhere both Marx and Engels frequently refer to the subjection of females by males, of the oppression of women by men, and even of the slavery "latent" in the family, they only once remark, and that in passing, that marriage as we

---

11. *Origin of the Family, Private Property, and the State* (International Publishers, N.Y., 1972), II.3:

The overthrow of mother right was the *world-historic defeat of the female sex.* The man seized the reins in the house also; the woman was degraded, enthralled, the slave of the man's lust, a mere instrument for breeding children. . . .

and 11.4,

. . . this (the monogamian family) is based on the supremacy of the man; its express aim is the begetting of children of undisputed paternity, this paternity being required in order that these children may in due time inherit their father's wealth as his natural heirs.

have come to know it, (and as they specifically discuss it in terms of monogamous marriage), in fact converts women and children into forms of private property owned by their husbands and fathers.

Sex Inequality and Class Inequality

There is, however, an indication that the precise status of women in terms of property relation was a problem for them. In the *German Ideology*, it is stated that "this latent slavery in the family, though still very crude, is the first property."[12] And in the *Economic and Philosophic Manuscripts of 1844*, in his discussion of "crude and thoughtless communism," Marx states that:

> [In its first form, communism counterposes universal private property to private property which] finds expression in the bestial form of counterposing to *marriage* (certainly a *form of exclusive private property*) the *community of women*, in which a woman becomes a piece of *communal* and *common* property.[13]

But in the *Origin* Engels rejects the earlier position that women were the first form of private property and, in my opinion rightly, sees that it was the emergence of private property in the form of land and chattels under male ownership which was the first form of private property, and that it was the need to establish determinate inheritance rights regarding property of these types which led to the subjection of women. However, in rejecting the possibility that women were the first form of private property he seems to have been led to deny that they were private property at all and consistently makes the subjugated position of women relative to men an *analogous*, or parallel, development with developing class antagonism. At *Origin* II.4 he says that,

> The first class antagonism which appears in history coincides with the development of the antagonism between men and women in monoga-

---

12. *German Ideology*, A.1.
13. *Economic and Philosophic Manuscripts of 1844, op. cit.,* p. 99.

mian marriage, and the first class oppression with that of the female sex by the male . . .[14]

But he does not say, as he should have, that the oppression of females by males is *itself* a class oppression expressed in a property relation. Since the form of marriage which developed was necessary for the preservation of exclusive male ownership of private property, women were the first exploited class. They were the first group of persons to be denied rights of ownership in private property and, hence, to be denied equal rights of access to ownership of the means of production. This sexual restriction on rights of property ownership was expressed in the marital and familial relation by making women the property of fathers or husbands. The legal status of women within marriage was that of a chattel;[15] they had a legal obligation to obey their husbands, no right to absent themselves from a husband's bed and board no matter how physically abusive his treatment of them, no right to any form of remuneration for their labor, no right to share in the ownership of matrimonial assets or to own even that property they brought with them into the marriage, and no rights of sexual or reproductive control. Their central conjugal duty was to honor the sexual and reproductive demands of their husbands, and failure to do so was grounds for dissolution. The "femme sole," spinster or unmarried woman, remained the property of her father or other male member of the family though she did have a right to inherit and to own property, a right made necessary by the fact that women were occasionally the only remaining heirs and their welfare had to be provided for if they failed to obtain husbands. This was, however, commonly accomplished through some form of trust over which the woman had no direct control and under which she was merely a third party beneficiary. It is precisely because Marx and Engels did not see that women were *denied* rights of ownership in familial property that they did not

14. *Origin, op. cit.*, p. 129.

15. See for example the comments made by the venerable scholar R. E. Megarry in *A Manual of the Law of Real Property,* 2nd ed. (London, 1955), p. 538.

see the oppression of women as a class oppression and did not recognize the fundamentally exploitative nature of reproductive labor.

It is my contention that they did not see this because they still adhered to a belief in the natural association of the sexes which led to a "natural" division of labor between them such that men "naturally" came to control the means and surplus of production and women "naturally" came to be responsible for the labor of reproduction. Thus, they had what might be termed a concept of the *partial* socialization of relations between the sexes. Even though they believed that women were unfairly treated because of their limited access to production, they saw this limitation as grounded partly in a natural division of labor between the sexes and partly in the exploitative marital relation necessary to provide a mechanism for cross-generational transfers of private property. What Marx and Engels did not fully acknowledge was the central importance within this system of (1) maintaining private property under exclusively male ownership, and (2) the exploitative nature of reproductive labor itself. As a result, they failed to appreciate the significance of the fact that the marital relation was itself a property relation.

This is striking. It would seem that a theory of historical change which took property relations as articulating the substructure of the basic and most fundamental determinants of social life and individual consciousness would be particularly careful to elucidate the kinds of property relations which existed, and to acknowledge the importance of property relations not merely between persons, but between persons such that members of one group literally owned members of another group. It is clearly one thing to exercise coercive control over others through denying them access to ownership of the means of production, but a different and much deeper thing to convert others into the kinds of things which not only cannot come to own other things, but which cannot own even themselves. In his account of the origins of the inequality of women through the emergence of the monogamous family under private property, Engels acknowledges that the private property which emerged was under male control. What he offers by way of an explanation of this is that the "natural" division of labor in the family led to men's control of the fields, the cattle, and other aspects of life which we think of as belonging to the "productive" rather

194

than the reproductive realm. Hence, men came to be in possession of the surplus arising from production, as it were accidentally. But quite apart from the fact that anthropological evidence suggests that a strict sexual division of labor follows rather than precedes the emergence of private property,[16] even if this could be said to explain how men came to be in *possession* of the surplus, it does not explain why it *remained* under their exclusive control. It does not in itself explain how or why males acquired *sole rights* of ownership over it. The structure of marriage which developed provides the explanation as to *how* exclusive male ownership was ensured, and how males institutionalized the appropriation of women's labor. But what still requires explanation is *why* they appropriated sole rights of ownership over the surplus of production. While Engels recognized that it was the fact that property arising from a surplus in production had emerged under male control that caused "the world historical defeat of the female sex," his explanation as to why it caused it does not do the job. There is nothing in the nature of private property itself which necessitates that it must pass through the paternal rather than the maternal line. Devising a structure of marriage which would ensure certainty of paternity for the purpose of inheritance provided an adequate mechanism for cross-generational property transfers. But it was not the only possible mechanism. This was the method chosen because males wanted to remain in control of the private property arising from the surplus in production. They did not deny women rights of ownership because they had to, but because it was in their interest to do so. It was because they appropriated sole rights of ownership to private property that it was necessary also to appropriate women's labor, both paid and unpaid. And it is as a result of that appropriation that women's labor became restricted to that of reproduction and that "reproduction" came to include not only the labor of childbearing and nursing, but child-*rearing* as well. Ensuring that women would perform the labor of rearing children both freed men from the necessity of sharing in this unproductive labor and ensured their continued ability to retain sole ownership of private property. Women simply lost out in the first round of dividing up the potential profits arising from expanding relations of produc-

---

16. See for example, Kelly-Gadol, *op. cit.*

tion. The inescapable fact has to be faced that males did appropriate sole rights to the ownership of property; even if women's unique biological capacities with respect to childbearing can be said to lie at the basis of the fact that males came to be in possession of the first forms of private property, it does not and cannot explain how males came to remain in the dominant position with respect to ownership and why they denied women rights of ownership even in themselves.

Thus while the Marxist premise still holds that the material conditions governing the production and reproduction of life are the fundamental determinants of both social life and individual consciousness (if one accepts the premise that inequality between the sexes arose following the emergence of private property), it cannot be maintained that the sexual inequality found under capitalist relations of production is superstructural. Of course, the *mythology* of male supremacy is ideological and superstructural. But it is necessary because it supports the basic structure of property relations and of the division of labor *between the sexes,* and *not* because it supports the basic structure of property relations between classes of men. The doctrine of male supremacy is indeed both ideological and superstructural. But what Marx and Engels did not recognize is that there is a property relation as between the members of one sex and the members of the other, and that, as a property relation, it is part of the substructure of social relations.

Further, since the specific form of the property relation between men and women was one of ownership of the latter by the former, this determined that women's position would be fundamentally different from men's and that this was, and would continue to be, substructurally determined. This is why women cannot be fitted into the Marxist analysis, cannot be independently assigned a class position, and cannot have their labor of reproduction counted as "labor."

Since the ideological superstructure of male supremacy supports the basic substructural property relation existing *between the sexes* rather than between classes of men, sexual inequality is not a *product of* class inequality. Rather, class inequality, in the sense in which Marx and Engels explicated and used it, was a further development of sexual inequality. The first inequality which arose following the emergence of private property was sexual inequality—inequality in the dis-

196

tribution of rights of ownership as between the sexes. The ideological construct of women's allegedly "unique" relation to reproduction was necessary to ensure continued exclusive male rights of property ownership, to justify sexual inequality in the attribution of rights of ownership, and to rationalize women's enforced reproductive servitude. Women's inferior status is a function of their disadvantaged position in relation to *both* production and reproduction—a direct result of that first sexual inequality, inequality of property *rights*.

Class inequality is inequality in the distribution of property as between males who are differentially determined by their specific relation to the means of production. There could be no unique class inequality in the sense in which Marx and Engels were concerned with it—that is, as between individual men and ultimately classes of men—unless there had already been a prior stage of development in which it was established that only men had rights of ownership, that only men had independent class membership. Sexual inequality can thus be seen within Marx and Engels' frame of reference as itself a class inequality, indeed the first class inequality.

Under the form of marriage which developed following the emergence of private property, men had sole rights of control over women's sexuality and reproductivity. As well as ensuring certainty of paternity for the purpose of inheritance and exclusive male ownership, this also ensured that necessary, *socially* necessary, reproductive labor would be performed. That it was performed as a "private" function, for the benefit of individual men, does not change the fact that it also accomplished the end of ensuring that future individuals would be produced for the benefit of society. But an understanding of the fact that this is how reproductivity was ensured makes it clear that Marx and Engels were simply wrong, or were wrong about half the population, in claiming that the fundamental determinants of human consciousness arise from the relations of individuals to the modes of production. That is true for men only, and requires modification even there. But insofar as it is clear that women, as forms of private property, had an *exchange* value, and that this value was determined primarily by their sexual and reproductive capacities, it is also clear that the position of women, and their consciousness, were fundamentally determined not by their relation to production, but by the demands of reproduction, and, indeed, of a specific form of reproduction made subservient to a system of property distribution designed to preserve exclusive male rights of ownership and certainty of paternity.

It is not, then, the *real* relationship of woman to reproduction which determined both her position and her consciousness. It is rather her relation to reproductivity *under* this specific system of property regulation and distribution, and in terms of the reproductive ideology and mythology appropriate to this system, which are the determining factors. It is a requirement of this system of property distribution, and a central tenet of its reproductive mythology, that women have a "unique" relation to reproduction. This mythology is then used in turn as a ground for her role as a reproductive laborer and her unsuitability as a member of the productive, public, property-owning world. Women are determined by reproduction, not because there is any reason in nature why their biological capacities should thus limit them, but because their ideologically construed relation to reproduction is used to justify placing and keeping them in enforced reproductive servitude through the marital relation. This ideology is very powerful indeed. There can be no question at all that it determines the consciousness of women, and men's consciousness of women's consciousness. Marx and Engels failed to appreciate the extent to which the relation between women and reproduction was ideological and so they failed to see that women's historical position as reproductive laborer was an exploited one arising from the fact that they were denied the rights both to determine the form of their labor and to own its products. Thus the historical fact was not simply that women were so busy at home that they could not work, but rather that they had to be forced to stay at home in order to ensure that necessary reproductive labor was performed and the rights and privileges of the dominant owner sex preserved. And the desire to keep them as involuntary reproductive laborers was the primary motive for denying them access to the productive labor market. The ideology of motherhood is simply part of the superstructure whereby dominant sex–class position is maintained.

Theoretical Implications of the Property Relation Between the Sexes

Thus class society as we know it, and as Marx and Engels explained it, developed out of sexist society. The first stage determined 1) that males, and only males, could and would be potential owners of private property, and 2) that women would do reproductive labor. The second stage determined that only some males would be actual owners of private property in forms other than women and children. However, from the fact that any man can have a wife and children, it is clear that no matter how disadvantaged a man is, as determined by his relation to the mode of production, all men may choose to own property in the form of wives and children, and the exercise of this choice is in no way affected by their specific relation to the mode of production.[17] Once it is recognized that there is a very specific property relation between the sexes it is clear that sexual inequality is sub- rather than super-structural and that this fact will produce different results than would be produced if this property relation did not exist. An account of the processes of historical change which neglects the role of this property relation will necessarily fail to give a true account of how

17. It is worth pointing out that the degree to which men feel compelled to marry, and to marry the particular women they do, is perhaps a rough measure of their assessment of how successful they will be in acquiring private property which will have to be passed on. Clearly, individual men need to marry and sire offspring if and only if they are going to have property to worry about. Thus, this system of property distribution historically determined men as well as women, though hardly to the same extent. But to the extent that marriage and fatherhood are also experienced by men as involuntary and alienated, this is to be explained by reference to its place within this system of property distribution and the historical methods chosen to perpetuate it. It is precisely because the necessity of biological inheritance has been overcome as the only available mechanism of achieving property transfers across generations that even members of the dominant sex-class can now countenance and even welcome women's release from reproductive servitude. But it is also this fact that makes the central problem clear: if women are released from compulsory reproductivity, how can we ensure that the socially necessary labor of reproduction will be performed?

and why it is that private property is differentially distributed between men and women as well as between classes of men, and of how and why it is that labor is differentially distributed between the sexes.

Marx and Engels were completely right in seeing that traditional political theory systematically provided a justification for a system in which the distribution of private property was characterized by inequality. But Marxism has utterly failed to account for the fact that sexual inequality as much as inequality within the male community is a dominant characteristic of the traditional system of property distribution. It does not provide an explanation as to *why* traditional political theory assumed that all potential owners were male. Further, because Marx and Engels did not notice (or did not think it significant) that the relation between the sexes was a property relation, they also failed to notice or to pay sufficient attention to the fact that reproductive labor was in fact extorted from women.

The reason Marxism does not see this systematic justification is that Marx and Engels concentrated their efforts on showing that *individual* inequality of ownership was the cause of capitalism's class inequality rather than observing that the emergence of private property accounted for *both* the systematic justification of class inequality *and* for the sexual inequality itself. They simply did not acknowledge that the system they were out to attack was based on sex dominance as well as class dominance. A dominant sex was created when women were denied rights of ownership and converted into private property with a primarily sexual and reproductive function. A dominant class *of men* was created when men were differentially determined by their specific relation to the means of production. And a dominant form of labor was created when reproduction was made subservient to the demands of private property as controlled by men. To the extent that Marxism acknowledges women's historical position as exploitative and unjust it may be argued that Marx and Engels were aware of the sexual inequality in property rights. However, to the extent that Marx and Engels traced this inequality to physiological or biological factors rather than to woman's involuntary relegation to the reproductive

200

realm, they, too, espoused an ideological view of reproduction.[18]

To their credit, Marx and Engels believed that sexual inequality could be remedied. But their analysis is incomplete. Merely allowing women access to the sphere of production is not enough. Sexual inequality in the sphere of reproduction must also be remedied.[19] The

---

18. Despite the humanism and compassion apparent in so much of Marx's writing about the relation of the sexes, it is apparent that he held a "natural" view of the association between the sexes, particularly in relation to procreation. As he says in the *Economic and Philosophic Manuscripts of 1844, op. cit.*, pp. 100–101:

In the approach to *woman* as the spoil and handmaid of communal lust is expressed the infinite degradation in which man exists for himself, for the secret of this approach has its *unambiguous*, decisive, *plain* and undisguised expression in the relation of *man* to *woman* and in the manner in which the *direct* and *natural* procreative relationship is conceived. The direct, natural, and necessary relation of person to person is the *relation of man to woman*. In this *natural* relationship of the sexes, man's relation to nature is immediately his relation to man, just as his relation to man is immediately his relation to nature—his own *natural* function.

But what is his and her, "natural" function? And what is this "natural" relation and association? Given that Marx is so clear that it is partly a matter of how the relation is *conceived* that provides a measure as to how far it demonstrates the essential aspects of man, what is it that he conceives of as being so clearly and distinctly "natural" and "direct"? Is this "association" marriage, or something else? What does it entail in terms of the rights and responsibilities it generates if its procreative potential is realized? Even if it is a natural association, does this mean that it is any the less in need of regulation to ensure mutuality and reciprocity than any other social relationship? Certainly he seems to assume that the basic relation between man and woman is procreative, or at least that this is what is most "natural" and "direct" about that relation, and surely that is open to question. Despite the generosity of spirit that comes through in this passage, it certainly isn't clear what he thinks follows from this natural association, or what it is about it that is natural. Nor should we assume that what is "natural" is necessarily desirable.

19. The primary rights claimed by men under the system we have enjoyed up to now were rights to female sexuality and reproductivity. I need hardly say how much needs to be said, hence, about the alienation of women from

essential point which must be acknowledged is that Marx and Engels did not recognize the difference between the historic positions of women and men. It is thus impossible to say whether they chose to explain women's inferior status as a "natural" outgrowth of their relation to reproduction because they simply failed to notice the specific property relation between the sexes or because they preferred *not to emphasize* this specific relation and *not to see* dominant sex ownership and the sexual division of labor as problems. For whatever reason, Marx and Engels, along with their predecessors and, until our own time, their successors, assumed that rights of ownership were "naturally" an exclusively male function and did not acknowledge that this right was maintained by the denial of rights to women.

Implications for Development of Theory Relating Productive and Reproductive Labor

Within the structure delineated by Marxism, collective ownership of the means of production is restricted to those who are related to the mode of production. Those who are not directly related to the mode of production have no right to property even under collective ownership. For practical purposes this means that women will, on the whole, be denied rights to the ownership, or more strictly speaking, to

---

the labor of reproduction. Most women are acutely aware, at least at some level, that they have not had a right to determine their own labor. They are aware either that they were not free not to choose reproductive labor, or that even if they did "freely" choose it, that they did not determine its nature and circumstances. I would suggest that there is a direct correlation between positive feelings about reproduction and having had relative freedom to choose to engage in reproduction and between negative feelings about reproduction and having had no sense of being free to pass it up. Doubtless there are also some in the "positive" camp who are still suffering from ideological "reproductivitis." But awareness that reproductive labor has been exploited labor must not blind us to the fact that it *need* not be exploited and that the kind of persons a society produces, and the way it produces them, are major moral and political issues. For discussion of these and related issues the reader is also directed to Mary O'Brien's, *The Politics of Reproduction* (London: Routledge & Keegan, 1981).

control of the means and products of production. A clearer way of putting this is to say that all those who are exclusively engaged in reproductive labor have no access to control of the means of production. Thus women can acquire property (whether under individual or collective ownership) *only at the expense of reproduction.*

We must ask both whether women feel this is justified and, perhaps more importantly, whether society can afford to take such a view. A complete theory of social relations must include an account of how society ensures there will be a future society; it must provide a framework and justification for a specific system of reproductive relations. Marxism does not do this. Beginning from the assumption that the inferior status of women is at least partly a result of a physiological difference between the sexes with respect to reproduction, it sees the remedy for the problem of reproduction in such things as communal day-care centers, bath-, wash-, and meal-houses, and that is as far as it goes. But even though that is a step in the right direction, it does not go nearly far enough. Making it easier for women to go to work does not ensure sexual equality because the assumption remains that women are primarily responsible for reproduction. Until men are the equal of women in relation to reproduction, women cannot be the equals of men in relation to production. The real issues that must be faced are who is to determine the ultimate shape and form of society? How would social forms have to change in order to ensure equal sexual determination in relation to reproduction? Who has the right to rationalize what may well be the conflicting demands of reproduction and production? Who is going to decide when and under what conditions women will bear, even if they cease exclusively to rear, children? Insofar as women have any unique relation to reproduction, ought not they, and they alone, to have rights of reproductive autonomy?

In brief, how can we ensure sexual equality without first developing a structure within which both productive and reproductive labor are seen to be essential social tasks necessitating a distribution of authority and the attribution of rights necessary to ensure that both tasks are adequately attended to without subordinating the rights of reproductive laborers to the demands of productive labor or vice versa? While Marxism has succeeded in articulating a theory of egalitarian relations of production, it has not even begun to articulate a theory of egalitarian relations of reproduction. A complete political, social, and economic theory would do so and would also provide a procedure for resolving potential disputes between what may be the competing demands of reproduction and production.

Marxism fails to see that political theory has articulated a particular reproductive mythology as well as a particular productive mythology. The dialectic begun with the emergence of private property can end only with sexual equality in the ownership and control of the means and products of both production and reproduction, with sexual equality in the distribution of both productive and reproductive labor.

While collective ownership of the means and products of production is the means to productive equality, at least where it is assumed that all persons are members of the productive labor force, collective ownership of the means of reproduction is not the means to reproductive equality.[20] The task for socialist theory is to develop a theory of collective ownership of the *products* of reproduction (children) which assumes that all persons are members of the reproductive labor force.

---

20. This is explicitly acknowledged by Marx, for example in the *Economic and Philosophic Manuscripts of 1844, op. cit.*, pp. 99–101.

9
THE MAN QUESTION

Judith Hicks Stiehm
University of Southern California
Los Angeles, California

The Man Question
Judith Hicks Stiehm

Introduction

For centuries men have read, written and taught political thought. They have done so with scant attention to women as authors, audience or even subject. Then, in the nineteenth and early twentieth centuries democratic theory emerged as *the* legitimating explanation of government. Then, upper class women began to realize that they possessed the qualities (other than biological) possessed by lower-class men. The latter were gradually being admitted to political life; the women were not. Some began to insist that their property, experience and education entitled them to political participation too. Finally theorists began to ask "What do women want?" and to debate "The Woman Question." Today it seems appropriate to go further and to consider Western political thought as an expression of "what men wanted." By giving conscious attention to "The Man Problem" or "The Man Question," it may be possible to shape a political theory which incorporates the experience of both women and men and their private and public lives.

Men's special connection to governmental force and women *and* men's connection to each other, to their relatives of several generations and to those around them are the continuing themes of this essay. They are developed around three assumptions men have made about govern-

Mark Kann dissected an early version of this essay.

ment which are so fundamental as to go mostly overlooked. When each of these assumptions is discussed in terms of women and government they acquire visibility. They become accessible to inquiry. The first concerns government as having a geographical definition—the assumption is that citizenship is defined by territory and that public relationships, those between citizens, are appropriately different from the private relationships of people who are related to each other, i.e., who are kin. The second assumption concerns changes over time—the assumption is that institutions (such as states and estates) should endure even though people cannot. The third assumption concerns government as legitimate force—the assumption is that governments may require male citizens to punish, jail and kill other citizens and also noncitizens.

Space: Citizens and Kin

Western political thought describes governments as composed of persons. But governments also have specific geographic boundaries, and jurisdiction over particular persons is first and foremost spatial. Why, then, have so many men been so serious about contract theories of government which describe states as composed of persons? Perhaps because all men have considered themselves at least potentially political for some time. This would suggest that women, who were excluded from governing theory but who have been included in governmental jurisdiction, have a clearer sense of the geographic determinism of citizenship and hence of the qualified nature of a citizen's voluntarism.[1] Indeed, empirical studies which show women have a lower sense of political efficacy than men may reflect the fact that women *are* less efficacious, but it is also possible that women have a more accurate picture of the political process than men. One "man

---

1. If women had ever been mere household members the state would have had only indirect jurisdiction over them, i.e., through the head of their household. In fact, the state has always presumed to directly regulate women's behavior, sometimes even in such personal considerations as dress. For women the state was not a confederation of citizens to which they had no relationship, but a federal government which directly affected them although they could affect it only indirectly.

question," then, is why do men emphasize the state as composed of consenting people instead of persons encompassed by a specified territory? Also, does men's emphasis on citizen autonomy lead to an inflated (perhaps even dangerous) belief in national sovereignty or national autonomy? Doesn't geography severely constrain the political possibilities of both nations and individuals?

Mapping is fundamental to statecraft. This means an individual's physical location and birth location are crucial influences on that person's political options. When outside the territory of their citizenship individuals may call on their home governments for protection, but they are keenly aware that the government of their physical location is likely to determine their fate. Conversely, citizens opposed to their government are often forced to leave their countries. Those with few resources and little hope of returning are usually referred to as refugees; those with resources and hopes of returning are often termed exiles. Geographical displacement of this kind is demoralizing and draining.[2] Any discussion of citizens and families, of the public and the private, must be undertaken, then, in the context of a geographic boundedness that does not provide for free movement. Every nation restricts movement into its domain; some restrict movement within and some restrict emigration as well. That population movement which does occur frequently occurs despite governments.

Precious as citizens may hold their lives, governments hold their territory dearer. Thus, citizens' lives are regularly sacrificed for space; land is almost never ceded nor is secession provided for. Geography appears clearly prior to citizenry.

Perhaps men's tendency to gloss over the political determinism of geography reflects their greater freedom (as compared to women) to move both within countries and across national frontiers.[3] Whatever

2. See Fanny Tabak, "Women and Authorian Regimes," in this volume.

3. For informal restrictions on women's freedom of movement see Susan Brownmiller, *Against Our Will* (New York: Bantam Books, 1976). Formal restrictions include laws which forbid a woman to leave the country without the specific permission of her spouse. See, "Symposium on Law and the Status of Women," special issue of the *Columbia Human Rights Law Review*, Vol. 8, No. 1, (1977): 144.

the reason, place remains a governmental essence. Indeed, some argue that government begins precisely at the point when a society creates coercive rules which are to apply not to kin but to all those within a particular geographic area.[4] Thus, Athens could be said to have become a government at the end of the 6th century B.C. when the "tribes" on which government was organized were given a new and geographic definition instead of the traditional, kin-based definition.[5]

Everywhere duties said to be owed family differ from those said to be owed nonfamily. This is true even when non-kin are present and family members absent. (Governmental values emphasize similarity and justice; familial values include favoritism and acceptance.)[6] When mobility and/or increased density bring non-kin into regular contact, it is convenient to have a government which can enforce rules guiding their interaction. But special, familial obligations are not necessarily ended by nor are they necessarily compatible with civic obligations. *Antigone* reminded the ancients, and the feud or vendetta continues to influence people today. Honor, especially family honor, has compelled, still compels and will probably continue to compel both nonutilitarian and illegal behavior.[7]

States do not usually recognize family ties as overriding; in practice, though, they recognize that few citizens treat their neighbors as they treat their relatives. It is easy to see that benefit can be derived from

---

4. See Hartsock's essay in this volume and Lucy Mair, *Primitive Government* (Baltimore, Maryland: Penguin Books, 1966), pp. 9–18.

5. Spatial control has never been absolute—strong powers have forced weaker ones to grant extraterritoriality to their citizens; in medieval towns different organizations such as religious orders and universities claimed governing authority over their members; and, conversely, some families have held governmental power, as is the case in Saudi Arabia today.

6. For an elaboration see Judith Stiehm "Government and the Family: Justice and Acceptance" in Virginia Tufte and Barbara Myerhoff, eds., *Changing Images of the Family* (New Haven: Yale University Press, 1979), pp. 361–375.

7. See Peter C. Dodd, "Family Honor and the Forces of Change in Arab Society," *International Journal of Middle East Studies* 4 (1973): 40–54. For a discussion of honor in U.S. culture see Bertram Wyatt-Brown, *Southern Honor* (Oxford: Oxford University Press, 1982).

having government serve as a dispassionate arbitrator between neighbors—and also between passionate family members.[8] But governments can provide another important function—that of limiting familial liability. Just as the creation of corporations limited financial liability without limiting possibilities for economic enterprise, governments can limit debilitating family responsibilities which might otherwise involve a wide circle of relatives and even span generations. Thus, governments can be described as 1) a way of escaping the literal rule of patriarchy, and 2) a way of helping patriarchs to escape having to be patriarchs! Again, an abused spouse can appeal to government, but a burdened husband can also obtain a no-fault, no-alimony divorce, refuse a loan to his impoverished uncle, and leave prosecution of his sister's rapist to the police. Because government rules over those "worth ruling," one is not dishonored by permitting it to act on one's behalf, nor is one dishonored by accepting its rule.[9]

Let us take private and public, then, to refer respectively to relationships defined by kinship and by territory. Then it becomes evident that both men and women always participate in both kinds of relationships. The idea that men hold sway in a public sphere and women in a private seems a patent if not pathetic attempt to create symmetry. Obviously both women and men are both private and public beings. Obviously, too, neither exercises much individual control in the public sphere (although virtually all women are excluded from government as opposed to only most men). Within the private sphere a variety of balances may be struck, but neither men nor women are without domestic power. Even in the specialized situation where the man has a substantial cash income and the women none, women (even Yeatman's harem members) have the power of an Afghanistan, Vietnam, or El Salvador—that based upon being there—that of occupation—that of existing in a particular space and of being prepared to stay in that space.[10]

There is some irony in the fact that women have so often been con-

---

8. Actually, police officers are reluctant to get involved in domestic disputes—because, among other things, they are considered most dangerous.

9. See Hartsock's essay in this volume.

10. See Anna Yeatman's essay in this volume.

signed to the private sphere, the sphere of kinship. Yes, it is true that the surest ties of kin are those between mother and child and between siblings of the same mother. It is also true that the energy and care given to providing men assurance of their paternity suggests the importance attached to parental ties.[11] Indeed, these ties are apparently so important that men have used government, a created, forceful institution to help guarantee them a relationship (that of a parent) women have always been able to take for granted.[12] However, even if women seem firmly embedded in the family, in another sense they are the outsiders, the nonmembers. Women may be the certain link between siblings of the next generation, but they are not blood relations of their husbands. (No donation of organs can be made between spouses.) The husband-wife tie is man-made (often by government), and it can be unmade. Spouse is the only kin relationship which can be undone. Neither parents nor children are divorcible. Spouses are chosen, other kin given.

For centuries it has been women who have left their families, taken another name, and served as a link (sometimes even as a hostage) to ally families who might otherwise be rivals if not enemies. The cement is, of course, not the marriage *per se* but the converging of two families' interests in the offspring. It is the creation of a joint stake in the future. In any "present" the wife is an outsider. Indeed, while it is men who tell mother-in-law jokes, it is women who most certainly experience the conflict and ambivalence created by their socially created ties to husbands who are also bound first and in a way which cannot be undone to their mothers. The one is a tie from the past; the other, though, represents the future. Ironically, then, women achieve cen-

---

11. With the advances in tissue typing developed for organ transplants it is now possible to determine an individual's paternity with almost the same assurance as maternity. This is wholly new; previously all that could be proven was some person's *non*paternity.

12. The sexes' different kinds of parenting are discussed in Dorothy Dinnerstein, *The Mermaid and the Minotaur* (New York: Harper & Row, 1977), Nancy Chodorow, *The Reproduction of Mothering* (Berkeley: The University of California Press, 1978), and Mary O'Brien, *The Politics of Reproduction* (London: Routledge and Kegan, 1981).

trality in the kin relationship in their children's generation. Men's natural centrality (as opposed to that created by society) comes in the
generation of his brothers.

A second "man problem," then, occurs because men cannot have
babies, must find wives who are not related to them, and lack assurance of the paternity of their wives' children. That problem often
causes men to try to restrict wives' (not necessarily women's) physical
space.[13] That space is the public, the space occupied by persons to
whom one is not related. Men have preferred to keep that space wife-
free. Public areas, then, are considered safe only for those women who
cannot become pregnant. One result of having limited public access is
to cut women off from government. Again, this occurs because government specifically regulates relations between non-related individuals and because it is precisely non-related individuals that men wish to
keep separate from the women of their family. In sum, men's fragile
link to parenting, to reproduction, leads them to try to curtail women's
access to the public, and, hence, to government.

The public sphere involves government; it is also the site of most
economic production. The reasons for confining women apply to both
activities and for the same reason—because they take place in public.
It is important to remember that women have always worked in production when it is done with relatives or when it is done with women.
They are often not allowed in production which is done with non-
related men. The problems women debate today about their participation in production (or more generally the paid labor force) are rooted
in the sex segregation of work. Any number of studies have sought explanations for this segregation. None has yet proven more satisfying
than this somewhat primitive formulation.[14]

To review, the political thought of Western man describes government as the purposive creation of men primarily designed to regulate
the relationships between non-related individuals. Women, who have

13. Single women, prostitutes, divorcees and old women have "space"
privileges wives of child-bearing age don't have.
14. The (U.S.) National Academy of Science is completing a major review
of this research. Write Dr. Heidi Hartman, National Academy of Science,
Constitution Avenue, Washington, D.C.

experienced government as willy nilly rather than as intended artifact, are more apt to grasp the territorial and non-voluntaristic nature of government. They know 1) they did not participate in the creation of their government, and 2) they are subject to a government because of where they were born or live. They also know that men share the private sphere of kinship with them and that many men try to restrict women from the public spheres of government and work where they would be in contact with non-related men. Clark seems right.[15] Men must be considered as husbands and fathers as well as citizens and workers if a social theory can hope to be complete.

Time: Generational Replacement and Displacement

In the home one commonly eats and sleeps; it is also there that one is most likely to relate both to the opposite sex and to persons of different generations—older and younger. Any private space such as a home is within (not separate from) public space. The relations within that private space, though, are quite different from those among citizens. They are richly differentiated, yet they are apparently simple enough (or common enough) to be explained to even the most language-poor anthropologist doing field research.[16]

Both men and women participate in the web of familial relationships. Mostly men participate in the pyramid of governmental power. The question is: is hierarchical and forceful organization necessary to government? Must any women who participate in government necessarily adopt the role(s) now played by men? Or does governmental organization take its shape because it is the work of only men? How would men and women respectively organize a society which did not have to take the opposite sex into account? Examples of single sex societies are few. Phillip Wylie offered a fictional account in *The Disappearance,* but in contemporary society there are only a few instances.[17] One is prisons. Prisons are organized by the inmates. This is done within a coercive and limited environment. Men seem to orga-

---

15. See Lorenne Clark's essay in this volume.
16. See Carole Pateman's essay in this volume.
17. Phillip Wylie, *The Disappearance* (New York: Warner Books, 1978).

nize under a leader in a hierarchical pattern based on domination, force and even rape. The latter is done to men by men who do not consider themselves homosexuals. (Apparently, rape is interpreted as a proof of power and masculinity even if the only available object is male!) Women's prisons, in contrast, tend to be organized as families. Women assume both "masculine" and "feminine" roles, but they encompass the whole range of relationships (mother, brother, aunt) involved in families; these roles involve substantially less force.[18]

The "band of robbers" metaphor for the state is as old as St. Augustine. The metaphor may not be explicitly male but it seems fair to say it is implicitly so. In fact, the focus on a forceful group contest for the control of material goods seems not only male but closely related to the concept of government as men have developed it. Robber bands and governments both involve organized efforts to control property and to keep it from others who would like to control it—who would like to displace the current holder. Neither organization plans for property disbursement; neither sees the future as benevolent and secure.

Succession is the crucial element here. Succession occurs in families, in property ownership and in governmental office. Because humans are mortal it is inevitable. But succession not only works differently in the three systems, it may be a different experience for women than for men.[19] Succession may be most visible in government. There it is assumed that the state should be immortal, but, because men are mortal, elaborate rules for succession are laid out; nevertheless, changes in leadership inevitably involve some degree of crisis. Also, succession can occur at any time or place and whether or not powerholders are prepared for or even expect it. A set of officials can be displaced by younger men, older men, or men of the same age. Men are competent to exercise governmental power at 25, 45, 65; there is no necessary order and but few age limitations. As many as three genera-

---

18. Paul Bohannan, "Riots and Pseudo-Families," *Science 80,* May–June, 1980, pp. 22 and 25.

19. In families it occurs biologically. Property succession is controlled by law.

tions can be in competition with each other simultaneously for the same office.

Aristotle described governments as composed of heads of families. A different scheme was described by Freud who saw government as an association of brothers who killed and ate their father.[20] (The brothers could themselves be heads of families.) The central governmental problem for Freud, then, was also that of succession. It is not preventable; replacement must occur. But, when succession occurs before it is necessary it is experienced as *dis*placement, not replacement. Displacement seems more likely when succession involves control—control over valuable household property or over governmental force. To win succession to head of government or to head of house, then, can be tempting enough to some men to lead them to seek premature succession.[21]

After one has succeeded, care must be taken that one is not oneself prematurely succeeded. (Note that the same word is used to mean "victorious" and "following.") Sometimes those near the top of an organization do not think it enough to simply hold power until they choose or nature forces them to relinquish it. Some try to sustain their control (or at least influence) past their passing.

Governmental institutions, in particular laws, are frequently designed for the purpose of carrying out one's will after one is gone. Again, perhaps because only the heir is physically apparent when a bequest is obtained, bequests often are thought of from the point of view of the inheritor. In fact, of course, bequests are designed to carry out the wishes of the dead. They are designed to give power beyond life—to offer a certain immortality.

For men time must go slowly. They must regularly consider themselves ready to succeed long before their fathers are ready to be replaced. Indeed, much of what we consider government must have

---

20. Sigmund Freud, *Totem and Taboo* (New York: Random House, 1960).

21. The Old Testament tells of patriarchal families and one can understand the restlessness of Joseph's eleven brothers. For younger men older men represent blocked opportunity. This becomes truly insupportable when it appears that still younger men may leapfrog to power over a generation which has waited (patiently or impatiently) for its "turn."

been created to provide for men's anxieties about succession—both that they would succeed and that they would not be too early succeeded.

Succession and control over the future seem to be experienced differently by women. First, few of them have control over the kind of property that requires the creation of government and protection from familial (or even nonfamilial) successors. In addition, generational succession is different for them. For women their children's succession can represent extension with reduced responsibility. For them children are seen as natural replacements; they are not perceived as displacers—as persons who have no life, no role, no place until one has gone. Women do not have to stop having children because their children begin doing so. Also, grandmothering is in some respects more satisfying than mothering.

Moreover, much of women's work is and always has been invested in objects (family members) that one could not hope or wish to keep. Women have always invested in things (children) which were not owned, which would grow and leave. Relinquishment has always been a part of women's work. Loss of the products of their reproduction did not lead to Marxist alienation, and perhaps "loss" is not even the right word, for women's investment in the persons of the next generation gives them something precious—a stake in the future. Even if that stake must be considered vicarious, it is real.

The difference between parents' vicarious participation in the next generation and the kind of participation a citizen enjoys when he is represented in government involves a difference between deriving satisfaction from another's act measured by that person's standards as opposed to judging another's act by one's own standards. It is a difference which is rooted in the ability to enjoy another's pleasure. It is not egoistic. It does not conform to the contract theorists' description of man.

Men can invest in the future as women do, but they also invest heavily in non-parenting work. Many of them create (or obtain from salary) objects. Objects are vulnerable. They can be stolen or consumed; they can also be saved or lent or bequeathed. The artificial or socially defined nature of men's production and products makes men anxious to protect not only their objects (products), but the circumstances and arrangements surrounding their work. Much that men do, then, is defensive; it is maneuver; it is non-productive. In fact, some elaborate "security" arrangements actually lead to violence. They turn out to be destructive, and, in wartime, to be destructive of women's work—their children, especially their young men. This problem, the deaths of young men in the name of security, will be discussed further in the next section.

In the past, women's investment in the future through children has assumed that men would share some of that stake—that they would have a commitment to the next generation; at the same time, though, it must be remembered that men of a younger generation are perceived by older men as rivals, displacers, threats. This leads one to wonder about the effect of small and temporary families which diminish older men's stake in younger men. What will be the consequences of having many adult males who feel threatened but who lack a parental stake in the next generation? Will women be able to make the necessary generational investment alone? Will their investment be adequate? Will we witness a new social division which will not be specifically male-female but rooted in those with and without offspring? Will that division result in different time orientations, and in different desires concerning the maintenance of control beyond death? In defiance of the principles of sociobiology which assume human beings have a powerful wish/need to contribute to the gene pool, upper-class families (which have the resources to do as they wish/need) are smaller. Perhaps they have simply chosen to produce "quality children."[22] It is also possible, though, that they have determined they can control the future more successfully either through institutions or protégées. Submitting to the roulette of genetics may just be too risky for the rich. Possibly upper-class men believe they can have more and more enduring power if they place their stake on a chosen, adult "son" or on an artificial creature—government. That way they can program the future; otherwise, they merely assist its development.

---

22. See the literature on family economics, e.g., Theodore W. Schulz, ed., *Economics of the Family* (Chicago: University of Chicago, 1975).

Force: Manly Behavior

The final overlooked assumption is that government appropriately exercises force. Not only does it use force on noncitizens; it uses it on citizens. More importantly, the state forces (conscripts) men to use force but refuses to let women use force. In effect, women are involuntarily, unilaterally disarmed and men are forced to kill for the government.

Let us be clear. Few women are clamoring to be armed. Few wish to apply government's force or feel any need to be able to forcefully defend themselves. But even if women see no need to use force themselves, it is not at all clear that they advocate that men relinquish all use of force. Certainly some women are pacifists and advocate that position for both women and men. Others, though, see force as "men's business" and avoid thoughts about and contact with it. This laissez faire perspective is sometimes expressed as indulgence—boys will be boys—let them have their games—they're only hurting each other. Most women, though, probably support the force men exercise for the government. Although they may prefer to think of war and law enforcement as activities for which they have no responsibility, most women believe those activities give them a protection which is both real and needed.[23] Women do not usually question the reality of criminals and enemies nor do they question force as efficacious. They are likely to do so only when protection fails or when its consequences appear burdensome and/or threatening. This occurs when protection becomes expensive, when security measures such as curfews, classification of information and trade restrictions become cumbersome, or when one's country's weapons become a danger because of storage and disposal problems, or when they provoke one's enemy to increase *its* weaponry or even to launch a preemptive attack. Some of these considerations are currently being debated. However, when criminals or enemies appear to be winning, the usual response is not to question force as a response but to try to mobilize more force. Usu-

---

23. Judith Stiehm, "The Protector and the Protected," in Judith Stiehm ed., *Women and Men's Wars* (Elmsford, NY: Pergamon Press, 1982), pp. 366–376.

ally women support such an effort; they contribute to it; indeed, some inevitably contribute directly, e.g., by joining the military or a resistance organization.

Wars which are ultimately won don't lead to much analysis. Wars which are lost do. In fact, governments which lose a war usually lose office, too. They are criticized on dozens of scores, but almost never are they criticized for having failed to use half the country's resources—women. In short, while women may not wish to sully their hands with force, there are few men willing to accept their participation in the exercise of force.

Why? Are women thought not competent? Do men simply want a monopoly on the legitimate means of force? What would happen if women routinely were able to use force? What would happen if men were forbidden to use it?

Women do kill. They kill babies and spouses. They kill by accident and for profit. What they do not do is kill legitimately. They do not kill with authorization; they do not kill as the representatives of others. They certainly do not kill on behalf of men.

Is there anything to be learned from this lack of symmetry? Is women's disarmament voluntary? Or, since the rules are made by men, is it consented to by women? Does lack of access to force make women more vulnerable? Women do receive men's violence. Some victims of rape become victims precisely because they are women; other women are abused by spouses; many are the victims of the random or strategic violence of war. Women's response to violence is usually 1) to try to evade it, 2) to suffer passively, or 3) to appeal to a male authority to intervene (forcefully if necessary). Recently women have developed a sense of needing to be economically independent of men.[24] One wonders, why, then, women seem to accept dependency in the realm of protection. Is women's disinterest in the instruments of force caused by their lack of imagination—their inability to grasp the advantage which accompanies a capacity to enforce? Or do women have a

---

24. Or at least of men related to them, since women's appeal for assistance in achieving independence has alternatively been to male employers or to a government composed principally of men.

coherent explanation as to why it is better (either for women or for society generally) to restrict the use of force to men?

These "women questions" are deeply buried. Perhaps they cannot even be exhumed until we have considered some more "men questions." Why do men so routinely use violence in their relations with each other? Why have men sought to depersonalize rather than eliminate violence? what is gained by developing monstrous weapons which can be used at such long distances that the consequences of one's act need not be acknowledged? What is the function of a government which forces men with no quarrel, no antagonism, to kill each other? Is government merely a device to escape responsibility? Have men created it to absolve themselves of monstrous deeds?[25] Why have men kept weapons from women? Because one does not give weapons to persons one is exploiting? Or because proliferation (i.e., arming the other half of the globe's population) would increase the level of violence without altering any balance of power? Or, are men reluctant to give weapons to women because men do not think women are reliable, predictable, trustworthy?

Or, does the reason reside within men? Western thought has described man as an egoistic, atomistic individual, or, if social, as economic exploiter or exploitee. Both liberal and Marxist streams of thought assume the need for governmental force. Moreover, both assume force will be applied by the very persons whose nature or situation makes the force necessary. This would seem to create a dilemma. But even if elements of truth reside in either or both accounts it is not at all clear that theories about "economic man" (which are generally seen as congruent with "political man") are good descriptions of human beings. What if political theorists had begun by constructing generic man based upon all that they knew about women? Wouldn't we speak quite differently about human nature? For instance, it seems to be literally impossible to sustain a discussion on women's rights without entering into a discussion about children. Could an atomistic

---

25. Reinhold Niebuhr in *Moral Man and Immoral Society* (New York: Scribner, 1932) and Carol Gilligan in *In a Different Voice* (Cambridge: Harvard University Press, 1982) discuss the effect of experience on ethical judgment.

scheme have been devised if women had been the unit of thought? Gilligan argues that women's very reasoning about ethics is different from that of men's because women understand people as connected, as having responsibilities toward each other, as anxious to avoid doing harm.[26]

Could it be that men do not fit the atomistic scheme very well either? Could it be that we have all been led astray by the bachelorhood of the contract theorists Hume, Hobbes and Locke, and the paranoia of Rousseau? Could it be that men's private personas are more essential to them and to society than has been thought? Could it be that most men are, in fact, reluctant to sacrifice themselves or to kill others whatever governmental legitimacy is bestowed upon such action? If men are not reluctant, why must soldiers be drafted? Why is basic training so brutal? Why is the military so coercive? Why must the appeal to manhood be linked to the killing of others? Is this, too, nothing more than an ugly attempt to achieve symmetry? Since women create life, do we assign men a monopoly on the taking of life and thus trap men and their manhood?

Wars are fought by young men, sometimes, it seems, at the behest of old men. They are told this is how they may win a place, earn an inheritance. Sometimes young men seem to fight to displace old men, to relieve them of authority and resources before they are ready to yield them. In each case, though, it is clear that the use of organized force, whether that of the outlaw, the revolutionary or the government *is* a "man problem." Men do most of the violence and they do it mostly to men. Is this the result of a patriarchy that is particular and mutable? Can men be made less dangerous? In particular can young men be made less dangerous? Can proof of manhood be detached from willingness to use force? Why is the concept of power so truncated in discussion?[27]

---

26. Gilligan, *op. cit.*
27. See Jane Jaquette's essay in this volume.

Conclusion

If men expect women to take their theories of government seriously they will have to consider the meaning of geographic boundedness both because it limits voluntarism and because it can create conflicts between (felt) familial and civic obligations. Second, more thought will have to be given to efforts to control succession. This involves consideration of 1) the appropriateness of efforts to control others (and resources) after one is gone; and 2) the special problem men have of being displaced. All human beings face replacement. Sometimes, though, government theories seem focused on denying or overcoming that necessary event. Finally, men must understand that women understand legitimate force quite differently than they. Women see it several steps removed. They see it exercised by another sex, mostly on another sex and in another place—often in another country! When it impinges on them, though, women may reveal assumptions quite different from those of men.

The essays in this volume converge. They bring women's experience to bear on traditional Western political thought—thought which has assumed men's, but only questionably human, experience. All the essays insist upon the connections between women and men, and the public and private. Some raise the issue of men's monopoly on legitimate, organized force; several consider the connections between generations and the different "stakes" of women and men. The particularity, the narrowness, of what has been taught as political theory now seems both unconscionable and unimaginable. To insist on connections, though, does not imply that all is so hopelessly interconnected that even comprehension is beyond our grasp. Indeed, women's marginality may advantage them when it comes to describing the limitations of current theory, the absurdity of a disconnected individual as the unit for analysis, and the particularity of hierarchical organizations based on force.

SUGGESTED READINGS

Suggested Readings

U.S. Publishers

Allen, Christine Garside. "Can a Woman Be as Good in the Same Way as a Man?" *Dialogue,* 534–44, 1971.

Allen, Christine Garside. "Plato on Women." *Feminist Studies II* 2–3, 131–38, 1975.

Anzaldua, Gloria and Cherrie Moraga, eds. *This Bridge Called My Back: Writings by Radical Women of Color.* Massachusetts: Persephone Press, 1981.

Benston, Margaret. "The Political Economy of Women's Liberation." *Monthly Review,* xxi 4 13–27, 1969.

Chaney, Elsa. *Super madre—Women in Politics in Latin America.* Austin: University of Texas Press, 1979.

Chodorow, Nancy. *The Reproduction of Mothering: Psychoanalysis and the Sociology of Gender.* Berkeley: University of California Press, 1978.

Clark, Lorenne M.G. "Privacy, Property, Freedom and the Family." *Philosophical Law.* R. Bronaugh, ed. Connecticut and London, 1976.

Clark, Lorenne M.G., and Lynda Lange, eds. *The Sexism of Social and Political Theory: Women and Reproduction from Plato to Nietzsche.* Toronto: University of Toronto Press, 1979.

Davis, Angela. *Women, Race, and Class.* New York City: Vintage Books, 1983.

Diamond, Irene. *Family, Politics, and Public Policy.* New York: Longman, 1983.

227

Eisenstein, Zillah R., ed. "Capitalist Patriarchy and the Case for Socialist Feminism." New York: *Monthly Review,* 1978.

Eisenstein, Zillah R. *The Radical Future of Liberal Feminism.* New York: Longman, 1981.

Elshtain, Jean Bethke. *Public Man, Private Woman.* New Jersey: Princeton University Press, 1981.

Firestone, Shulamith. *The Dialectic of Sex: The Case for Feminist Revolution.* New York: Bantam Books, 1972.

Freeman, Jo. *The Politics of Women's Liberation.* New York: Longman, 1975.

Frye, Marilyn. *The Politics of Reality: Essays in Feminist Theory.* New York: Crossing Press, 1983.

Hartsock, Nancy. *Money, Sex, and Power.* New York: Longman Press, 1983.

King-Farlow, J. and W. Shea, eds. *Contemporary Issues in Political Philosophy.* New York: Science History Publications, 1976.

Landes, Joan. "Women and the Public Sphere." *Social Analysis,* No. 16, forthcoming, December, 1984.

Latin American Perspectives. *Women in Latin America—an Anthology.* Riverside, California, 1979.

Lederer, Laura. *Take Back the Night: Women on Pornography.* New York: Morrow, 1980.

Mitchell, Juliet. *Psychoanalysis and Feminism.* New York: Pantheon, 1974.

O'Brien, Mary. *Politics of Reproduction.* Boston: Routledge, Kegan and Paul, 1981.

Okin, Susan Moller. *Women in Western Political Thought.* New Jersey: Princeton University Press, 1979.

Pateman, Carole. "The Disorder of Women: Love and the Sense of Justice." *Ethics,* 91, 20–34, October, 1980.

Pesca Tello, Ann, ed. *Female and Male in Latin America—Essays.* Pittsburgh: University of Pittsburgh Press, 1973.

Redstockings. *Feminist Revolution.* New York: Redstockings, 1975.

Rowbotham, Sehila, Lynne Segal, and Hilary Wainwright. *Beyond the Fragments.* Boston: Alyson Publications, 1981.

Russ, Johanna. *How to Suppress Women's Writings.* Austin: University of Texas Press, 1983.

Sapiro, Virginia. *The Political Integration of Women: Roles, Socialization, and Politics.* Urbana: University of Illinois Press, 1983.

Sargent, Lydia, ed. *Women and Revolution.* Boston: South End Press, 1980.

Stiehm, Judith, ed. *Women and Men's Wars.* New York: Pergamon Press, 1983.

Yeatman, Anna. "The Procreative Model: The Social Ontological Bases of the Gender-Kinship System." *Social Analysis,* No. 14, December, 1983.

Non-U.S. Publishers

Barker, Diane Leonard and Sheila Allen, eds. *Sexual Divisions and Society: Process and Change.* London, 1976.

Cardoso, Fernando Henrique. *Autoritarismo e democratização.* Rio de Janeiro: Paz e Terra, 1975.

Cheresky, Isidoro. "Les conflits à l'interieur des Etats à regime autoritaire et la mobilisation democratique." Paper, IPSA World Congress. Rio de Janeiro, 1982.

Clark, Lorenne M.G. "Politics and Law: The Theory and Practice of the Ideology of Male Supremacy." *Law and Policy.* D. N. Weisstub, ed. Toronto, 1976.

Collectif Des Femmes D'Amérique Latine et de la Caraibe. Mujeres—Des Latino-Americaines. Paris: Ed. des Femmes, 1977.

Delphy, Christine. "The Main Enemy: A Materialist Analysis of Women's Repression." *Partisans,* special issue, 'Liberation des Femmes,' Paris, 1970.

Duran, Maria Angeles. *Nuevas perspectivas de la mujer.* Madrid: University Autonoma de Madrid, 1982 (2 vols).

Gaiotti de Biase, Paola. *Questione femminile e femminismo nella storia della Republica.* Brescia, Italia: Morcelliana, 1979.

Gillespie, Charlie. "The Breakdown of Democracy in Uruguay: Alternative Political Models." Paper, IPSA World Congress. Rio de Janeiro, 1982.

Harding, Sandra and Merrill Hintikka, eds. *Discovering Reality: Feminist Perspectives on Epistemology, Metaphysics, Methodology and Philosophy of Science.* Dordrecut, the Netherlands: D. Reidel, 1983.

Jaquette, Jane. "La Mujer latinoamericana y la Politica: Paradigmas Feministas y investigaciones comparativas por culturas," in *La Mujer in Latinoamerica*. Mexico, 1975.

Kearns, D. "A Theory of Justice and Love: Rawls on the Family." *Politics*, Australia , 1983.

Lacoste, Louise Marcil. "Feminisme et Rationalite." *La Rationalite Aujourd'hui/Rationality Today*. Ottawa, Canada, 1979.

Lloyd, G. "Masters, Slaves, and Others." *Radical Philosophy*. Australia, 1983.

———. "Public Reason, and Private Passion." *Politics*. Australia, 1983.

Macciocchi, Maria Antonietta. "La donna 'nera' - 'consenso' femminile e fascismo." Milano: Fertrinelli, 1976.

———. *Les femmes et leurs maitres*. Paris: Christian Bourgois, 1978.

O'Donnell, Guillermo. Modernización y autoritarismo. Buenos Aires: Paidos, 1972.

———. "Estado y alianzas en la Argentina, 1956–1976," in *Desarrollo Economico*, 16 no. 64, enero-marzo, 1977.

———. "Tensiones en el Estado burocratico—autoritario y la cuestión de la democracia." *Estudios CEDES*, Buenos Aires, 1978.

———. "Las Fuerzas armadas y el Estado autoritario del Cono Sur de América Latina," XXV Reunião Anual do Grupo "Armed Forces and Society." Chicago, 1980.

Pateman, Carole. "Feminism and Democracy." *Democratic Theory and Practice*. Cambridge: Cambridge University Press, 1983.

———. "Feminist Critiques of the Public-Private Dichotomy." S.I. Benn and G.F. Gaus, eds. *Conceptions of the Public and Private in Social Life*. London: Croom Helm, 1983.

———. "The Fraternal Social Contract: Some Observations on Patriarchal Civil Society." Paper, Australian Women's Philosophy Conference. Adelaide, 1983.

———. "Women and Political Studies." *Politics*, (Australia), 1982.

Rendel, Margherita, ed. *Women, Power and Political Systems*. London: Croom Helm, 1981.

Sawer, M. "Women in Australian Parliaments—The New Era." *Current Affairs Bulletin*. Australia, 1982.

Sawer, M. and M. Simms. *Women and Politics in Australia.* London: Allen and Unwin (forthcoming).

Scutt, J. "Equal Marital Property Rights." *Australian Journal of Social Issues,* 1983.

Smith, Dorothy, "Women and Corporate Capitalism." *Women in Canada.* Marylee Stephenson, ed. Toronto: Don Mills, 1977.

Tabak, Fanny. *Autoritarismo e participação politics da mulher.* Rio de Janeiro: Graal, 1983.

————. "Political Socialization and Authoritarian Regimes." Paper delivered at the ECPR/IPSA Workshop. Lancaster, 1981.

————. "Women's Role in the Formation of Public Policies in Brazil." M. Rendel, ed. *Women, Power and Political Systems.* London: Croom Helm, 1981.

Tabak, F. and M. Toscano. *Mulher e Política.* Rio de Janeiro: Paz e Terra, 1982.

UNICEF. *Mulher, sociedade e Estado do Brasil.* São Paulo: Brasiliense, 1982.

Vitale, Luis. *Historia y Sociologia de la Mujer Latino Americana.* Barcelona: Fontamara, 1981.